THE GREAT UNIVERSAL STUDIOS HOLLYWOOD SCAVENGER HUNT

Second Edition

A detailed path through Universal Studios Hollywood

CATHERINE F. OLEN

The Great Universal Studios Hollywood Scavenger Hunt
Second Edition
A Detailed Path through Universal Studios Hollywood

© 2021 Catherine Olen

All Rights Reserved. No Portion of this book may be reproduced, stored in a retrieval system, or transmitted in any form or by any means – electronic, mechanical, photocopy, recording, scanning or other – except for brief quotations in critical reviews or articles, without the prior written permission of the publisher. Subject to permission under section 107 and/or 108 of the 1976 United States Copyright act. Requests for permission should be addressed to the publisher wwww.mousehangover.com. 949-234-7332

First paperback edition July 2021

ISBN 978-1-64822-024-1 (paperback)
ISBN 978-1-64822-025-8 (eBook)

Published by Mouse Hangover
www.Mousehangover.com

Please note: Every effort has been made to ensure the accuracy of information throughout this book. The information is believed to be accurate at the time of printing. The publish and author are not responsible for errors or omissions, for changes to details or the consequences of the readers reliance to the information provided.
Attraction closures or updates are not the responsibility of the publisher or author and cannot be guaranteed at the time of use of this book.

Readers are welcome to contact the publisher for comments, updates or questions.

About the Author

Catherine Olen has been visiting Universal Studios theme parks since she was a small child. Olen fell in love with the parks built through the imagination of founder Carl Laemmle and became an annual passholder in 1991 and has held an annual pass ever since.

Olen first traveled to Universal Studios Orlando at the age of thirty, immediately falling in love with the Florida parks. She has traveled to the Universal Studios Orlando theme parks each year since and now travels to Orlando several times a year to revel in the new attractions as well as the classic favorites.

Olen now shares her love of all things Universal in *The Great Universal Studios Orlando Scavenger Hunt*.

Come Check Us Out

Check out new books, video and news at
www.Mousehangover.com
Subscribe to Mouse Hangover
Instagram - @TheMouseHangover
Twitter - @Mousehangover
Facebook - @Mousehangover
@WDWScavengerHunt

YouTube – Mouse Hangover

Other books:

The Great Disneyland Scavenger Hunt
The Great Universal Studios Hollywood Scavenger Hunt
The Great Walt Disney World Scavenger Hunt

Dedication

To everyone who loves the movies and takes the time to spend time at Universal Studio Hollywood.

To everyone who helped me along this journey, too many to list individually, you are my heroes.

Lastly, my thanks to Carl Laemmle for the vision that created Universal Studios and all of the members of the Universal family who make each visit special

Contents

Introduction ix
History xiii

Entrance 1
    New York Street 4
    Pet's Place 7
    Secret Life of Pets: Off the Leash 12
    Paris Street 20
    Despicable Me: Minion Mayhem 22
    Super Silly Fun Land 27
    DreamWorks™ Theater Featuring Kung Fu Panda 29

Wizarding World of Harry Potter 36
    Zonko's Trick's and Jokes 37
    Honeydukes 38
    The Three Broomsticks 39
    Hog's Head 40
    Ollivanders 42
    Owl Post™ 43
    Dervish and Banges 44
    Gladrags Wizardwear 46
    Tomes and Scrolls Specialist Bookshop 46
    Flight of the Hippogriff™ 47
    Harry Potter and the Forbidden journey™ 49

Universal Studios Shows 55
    Special Effects Show 56
    Universal's Animal Actors 60

WaterWorld®	64
Springfield	67
Krusty Burger	69
Cletus Chicken Shack	74
Moe's Tavern	77
The Kwik-E-Mart	82
The Simpson's Ride	85
Lower Lot	**93**
Revenge of the Mummy	93
Jurassic World	95
Transformers: The Ride 3D	98
The World-famous Studio Tour	**101**
Answer Key	**125**

Introduction

Founder Carl Laemmle came to California and founded Universal Studios in 1915 when the studios were heading to the west coast to build their new empire in the sunny state of California. The two hundred thirty-acre studio included outdoor sets, as well as, primitive soundstages. This allowed the general public to watch the silent movies being filmed on the lot. For twenty-five cents, the audience could cheer the hero and boo the villain on the western sets built on the sprawling acreage.

By 1964, Universal Studios opened their doors to the public once more as a theme park, allowing guests to take a short tram tour, watch a wild west stunt show and eat at the studio commissary.

Today, Universal Studios has expanded the original vision of Carl Laemmle by immersing guests in every aspect of film making from visiting your favorite film locations to seeing 3-D special effects up close and personal.

Catherine F. Olen

How to use this book:

Your Universal trivia is broken down into three categories

- One star – Easier questions – Good for families with small children or first-time guests
- Two stars – Challenging questions – For returning guests and those with more time
- Three stars – Expert questions – For those looking for a real challenge or park experts

All of the questions found in this book have been verified by several Universal enthusiasts but I am aware that the décor of Universal Studios changes regularly. If there are changes, you can visit www.MouseHangover.com for current updates. If you have come across a change prior to me, please email me so the changes can be noted.

I hope you find your way through the Universal Studios theme park with new eyes and enjoy your hunt for the details every guest can experience.

Note: All content is subject to change without notice. Ride closures, construction, or overlays for the Halloween and Christmas holidays may alter the content temporarily due to park-wide decorations.

Trademarks:

This book uses Universal Studios copyrighted characters, registered trademarks, marks, and registered marks of NBC Universal. J.K. Rowling copyrighted characters, registered trademarks, marks and registered marks. Disney™ owned characters, registered trademarks, marks and registered marks. The Simpsons, a registered trademark of 20th Century Fox™ and Disney™ created by Matt Groening.

The Great Universal Studios Hollywood Scavenger Hunt

All reference to celebrity names, trademarks, marks and registers marks are the property of the governing body, Mousehangover.com is in no way affiliated with these entities.

All references to these properties are made solely for editorial purposes. Neither the author nor the publisher makes any commercial claim to their use, and neither is affiliated with Universal Studios or NBC in any way.

History

Any history of Universal Studios must begin with the founder, Carl Laemmle. Laemmle worked in the dry good industry until one day in Chicago, Illinois when Laemmle wandered into a nickelodeon and saw his first flicker. While there are no specific records of this part of Laemmle's life, the stories passed down through the years talk about how he stood outside a nickelodeon counting the house receipts for an entire day and, shortly after, purchased several nickelodeons for himself.

In 1909, Laemmle began his first film making endeavor with the Yankee Film Company with two partners. In the years that followed, Laemmle expanded his holdings with the Independent Moving Picture Company in New Jersey.

Word of mouth says that Laemmle changed the face of early film making by including screen credits for the actors seen in his films. Other film makers kept the identities of their actor's secret so they could interchange them at will. Laemmle found this would enhance the interest in his films greatly by making his actors and actresses known thus creating the first movie stars.

Catherine F. Olen

The Universal Film Manufacturing Company was incorporated in 1912 by Laemmle and his numerous partners. Universal Studios, a two-hundred thirty-acre studio, was opened in North Hollywood in 1915.

Almost immediately, the gates of Universal Studios were opened to the public where, for a mere twenty-five cents, fans could watch their favorite celebrities act out the latest film property.

In the early 1920's Universal acquired character actor Lon Chaney and with the completion of *The Hunchback of Notre Dame* and *The Phantom of the Opera*, had created two of Universal's biggest successes to date.

In 1928, Laemmle promoted his son, Carl Jr. to studio head and the young Laemmle was able to convince his father to move forward with sound pictures, thus bringing Universal Studios to a new era of film making. One of the first sound films, *All Quiet on the Western Front*, won Universal their very first Academy Award™ for best picture. Unfortunately for the spectators, this put an end to the use of outdoor sets and required the studios to take production inside sound stages to control the ambient noise.

In the 1930's and 1940's, Universal Studios created a name for themselves with a series of movie monster pictures including *Frankenstein, Dracula, The Mummy, The Invisible Man, The Wolfman* and the remake of *The Phantom of the Opera*. While they would go on to have immense success with other genres of film, Universal Studios would be forever dubbed Universal Horror.

Like so many other studios in Hollywood, Universal had their ups and downs but always continue to make movies that kept the audiences coming back for more.

It was not until 1961 that Universal would open its gates once more to the public, allowing them to tour the studio lot on buses. The bus tours would be short lived, with the use of trams taking over to create less noise on the busy backlot area. By 1967, Universal created the infancy of the theme park with a wild west stunt show accompanying the backlot tours.

It wasn't until 1976 that Universal Studios would premier an attraction so exciting it would propel them into the theme park we know today. The Jaws attraction that is still a part of the backlot tour created the thrill of coming face to face with Bruce, the shark from the 1974 blockbuster *Jaws*. Soon, Universal created the ice tunnel seen in *The Six Million Dollar Man*, the collapsing Bridge seen in *The Bionic Woman* and *Battlestar Galactica*. Each new attraction putting the guests right in the middle of the action. Another part of the excitement of the backlot tour was the possibilities of seeing your favorite stars during their work day.

While Universal Studios has endured as a movie making empire. The theme park makes Universal Studios Hollywood one of the most beloved of Los Angeles experiences.

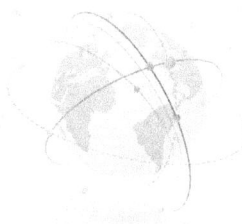

Entrance

Walk the red carpet and step through the gates of the largest movie studio in Hollywood. Enter a world where you will encounter alien battles, become a minion, fly on a broom or escape being eaten by dinosaurs.

While the entrance to Universal Studios Hollywood has changed dramatically over the years, the excitement felt by each guest has remained the same.

Back in the 1960's, Universal Studios opened a large building in this area as a welcome center for guests anxious to see a working movie studio. The only attraction available at the opening of the park was the studio tour, but this would make way for many more attraction in the future. Very quickly, a small animal actors show could be seen along with a wild west shoot out on the upper lot.

Throughout the decades, Universal Studios would grow to bring the latest special effects to the guests through interactive shows, rides and, of course, the studio tour.

Catherine F. Olen

1. ★★ As you enter the front gates of Universal Studios Hollywood, look around you. Find the bust of renown director Alfred Hitchcock. According to the bronze plaque on this bust, in what year was he born?
   a. 1915
   b. 1899
   c. 1900
   d. 1921

2. ★★ As you continue reading the plaque to Alfred Hitchcock, in what decade did the Alfred Hitchcock television show begin filming?
   a. 1960's
   b. 1940's
   c. 1950's
   d. 1970's

> **Did you know?**
> If you enter the guest relations building just behind the bust of Alfred Hitchcock, you will see movie posters and memorabilia from your favorite films and television shows.

3. ★★ Continue down the street and find the building facades to the left between the gift shops. As you stand before the Thalberg talent agency, on which days of the week do they hold auditions?
   a. Tuesday and Thursday
   b. Wednesday and Friday
   c. Saturday and Sunday
   d. Monday and Thursday

The Great Universal Studios Hollywood Scavenger Hunt

> ### Did you know?
> The Thalberg agency is a nod to producer Irving Thalberg who worked for Universal Studios for three years as studio manager. Known for Producing the Lon Chaney classic, *The Hunchback of Notre Dame*. Later Thalberg would go on to work with MGM studio. Thalberg was instrumental in starting the careers of such Hollywood legends as Lon Chaney, Clark Gable, Joan Crawford and Jean Harlow among countless others.

4. ★ As you read the sign for the Hollywood apartments, who will they *not* rent to?
   a. Singers
   b. Dancers
   c. Comedians
   d. Actors
5. ★★ In what year was the Jack Pierce makeup studio founded?
   a. 1915
   b. 1950
   c. 1925
   d. 1982

> ### Did you know?
> Meet your favorite animated friends from SpongeBob SquarePants, Trolls and Hello Kitty outside the Animation store to the right as you walk through the entrance area.

New York Street

Walk through a New York neighborhood where you can stop at the corner market or hang out on the fire escape and chat with your neighbors. Stop to greet the cop on the street or chat with the locals as they hang out of their windows to interact with the people down below.

6. ★★ On the corner of New York Street you will find the candy store. According to the air raid shelter sign on the building, how many persons does it hold?
   a. One hundred twenty-five
   b. One hundred fifty
   c. One hundred seventy-five
   d. Two hundred fifty

7. ★★★ As you read the headline of the New York Times in the newspaper box, what ties up midtown?
   a. Flood
   b. Rain
   c. Fire
   d. Wind

8. ★★★ If you read the New York Times carefully, how many new Gershwin songs were released?
   a. Fourteen
   b. Sixteen
   c. Twelve
   d. Seventeen

The Great Universal Studios Hollywood Scavenger Hunt

9. ★★ Which type of coins does the newspaper box not accept?
    a. Pennies
    b. Dimes
    c. Nickels
    d. Silver Dollars
10. ★★ As you find the box for the New York Post, what is the name of the centerpiece of the 1964 World's Fair?
    a. Sunsphere
    b. Unisphere
    c. Worldsphere
    d. Fairsphere
11. ★★ According to the photos on the front page of the New York Post, how many advanced tickets were sold for the fair?
    a. 10 Million
    b. 15 Million
    c. 28 Million
    d. 45 Million
12. ★ You will find a taxi cab on the street. How much does the first 1/5-mile cost you?
    a. $1.25
    b. $2.25
    c. $4.50
    d. $.95
13. ★ As you read the sign on the taxi cab, what is it available for?
    a. In town calls
    b. City calls
    c. Out of town calls
    d. Country calls
14. ★★★ As you stand in this area of New York, look at the windows high above the stores. According to the sign for the Bradford Nelson fight, how much does a ringside seat cost?
    a. $50.00
    b. $5.40
    c. $3.30
    d. $540.00
15. ★★ On the window for the 14th Avenue Gym on the second floor, the tag line reads, "Be a _____."
    a. Champion
    b. Fighter
    c. Heavy Weight
    d. Contender
16. ★★ Find the store Saul & Sons delicatessen, they sell kosher meats and specialty _____?
    a. Bread
    b. Produce
    c. Desserts
    d. Salami

17. ★ According to the sign for Saul & Sons Delicatessen, what year was it established?
    a. 1946
    b. 1966
    c. 1976
    d. 1956
18. ★★ On the barbershop entrance, which of these does the sign not allow?
    a. Dogs
    b. Policemen
    c. Salesmen
    d. Customers

Pet's Place

Stop by Pet's Place and visit with your favorite characters from the *Secret Life of Pets* films. Join the gang as you explore the shops and ride along in Secret Life of Pets: Off the Leash. Visit the Pet's Store for your new Pet's gear so you are in style for your new owner.

19. ★ As you walk along Pet's Place, stop in front of the 24-hour Laundromat. In what year was this business established?
    a. 1926
    b. 1956
    c. 1936
    d. 1963
20. ★ Find the Let's Be Happy Preschool. What color is the ladybug between the words Happy and Preschool?
    a. Yellow
    b. Green
    c. Pink
    d. Purple
21. ★ Look in the window of the Let's Be Happy Preschool. What is the name of the child that drew the house?
    a. Tanya
    b. Vivien
    c. Abigail
    d. Brooke
22. ★ Continuing looking through the drawings hanging in the window of the preschool. What item did Paul draw?
    a. Horse
    b. Firetruck
    c. Dog
    d. Soldier

Catherine F. Olen

> ### Did you know?
> As you look at the drawings in the window, the name of the child that drew the dog is Liam. This is a mention to the child in *Secret Life of Pet's 2* and the dog is Max.

23. ★★ As you continue exploring the window of the preschool, look at the children's jackets hanging in the cubbies. What design is on the blue raincoat in Eowyn's cubby?
    a. Hearts
    b. Stars
    c. Puppies
    d. Flowers

24. ★ Next door to the preschool stands Nooshy's Books. What story is depicted in the window of this bookstore?
    a. Rapunzel
    b. Peter and the Wolf
    c. Little Red Riding Hood
    d. Goldilocks and the Three Bears

> ### Did you know?
> The Mac Guff Cinema at Pet's Place is a reference to Mac Guff Illuminations™ in Paris. This company is a part of Illumination Entertainment™ and is instrumental in bringing your favorite characters to life on the screen.

25. ★ At New York City News, you will find the items offered on the front of the awning. Which of these is not one of the items you see listed?
    a. Greetings
    b. Maps
    c. Internet
    d. Groceries

The Great Universal Studios Hollywood Scavenger Hunt

26. ★★ As you look through the items displayed in the window of New York City News, in what year was Big John's Peanut Butter established?
    a. 1987
    b. 1878
    c. 1887
    d. 1978
27. ★★ How many loads does the bottle of Wash Wizard contain displayed in the window or New York City News?
    a. Thirty-two
    b. Eighty-two
    c. Sixty-two
    d. Ninety-two
28. ★★ What sort of product is in the So Shiny package in the window display?
    a. Shampoo
    b. Toothpaste
    c. Hair spray
    d. Nail polish
29. ★ What is the flavor of the Jojo Ma's Jam in the window of New York City News?
    a. Strawberry
    b. Boysenberry
    c. Grape
    d. Blueberry
30. ★★ Find the magazine display outside New York City News. What is the cost for HouseBroke magazine?
    a. Free
    b. $7.99
    c. $12.99
    d. $1.99
31. ★★ In The Secret Life of Pots magazine, which page does the article *Which Houseplants are Better Listeners?* start?
    a. Twenty-one
    b. Twenty-three
    c. Twenty-two
    d. Thirty-two
32. ★ On the cover of Muttropolitan Magazine, at what event do the rescues strut their stuff?
    a. Leashball
    b. Furball
    c. Rubberball
    d. Hairball
33. ★ In the Big City Local Magazine, what is the name of the pet therapist advertising in this publication?
    a. Dr. Maria Elva
    b. Dr. Amanda
    c. Dr. Francis
    d. Dr. Ashley

34. ★★★ At the corner, at the front of the virtual queue for Secret Life of Pets: Off the Leash, you will find two newspaper boxes. Look at the yellow box, how much does the pizza delivery person job pay?
    a. Tips only
    b. $15
    c. $12
    d. Minimum wage
35. ★★ Continue looking at the classified ads. Under the education section, what sort of lessons are offered on the top of the third column?
    a. Dancing
    b. Tight rope walking
    c. Fire eating
    d. Juggling
36. ★★★ Under the section marked For Sale, look for the ad for the oil painting of the cat. What is the title of this painting according to the ad?
    a. Count Lasagna on Red
    b. Count Casanova of the Neighborhood
    c. Prince Fuzzy of the Pillow
    d. Sir Squishy at Rest
37. ★★ Read the ad for the cricket bats for sale. What does the advertiser suggest these would be good for if you do not play cricket?
    a. Watermelon smashers
    b. Kindling for your fireplace
    c. Protection from the zombie apocalypse
    d. Flat baseball bats
38. ★ Find the ad for the rare beanie bears. How much does the seller want for these rare collectibles?
    a. Ten dollars
    b. Fifteen dollars
    c. Seven hundred dollars
    d. One hundred fifty dollars

The Great Universal Studios Hollywood Scavenger Hunt

39. ★★ As you read the Soho Gazette in the blue newspaper box, what is the cost of this newspaper?
    a. A dollar
    b. Fifty cents
    c. Seventy-five cents
    d. Eighty-five cents

Did you know?

If you read the news stories for the Soho Gazette, you will notice all of the stories are related to the *Secret Life of Pets* films. Whether it is the white tiger seen in New York or the headline about the animal control truck fished out of the river, you will see all of your favorite stories from these adorable films.

Secret Life of Pets: Off the Leash

40. ★★ As you stand in front of the building for Secret Life of Pets: Off the Leash, what does the puppy on the sign hold in his mouth?
    a. A ball
    b. A leash
    c. A collar
    d. A squeak toy
41. ★ As you walk through the lobby of the apartment building, stop a read the notices. Which night of the week is the Treat N. Greet being held?
    a. Monday
    b. Friday
    c. Saturday
    d. Thursday
42. ★ Find the notice to all residents. What type of music does the co-op warn the residents to keep the noise at a minimum?
    a. Heavy metal
    b. Country western
    c. Rap
    d. Disco
43. ★★★ Find the advertisement for the Caterer needed for the puppy dinner party. What breed of dog does the advertisement reference?
    a. Saint Bernard
    b. Pomeranian
    c. Great Dane
    d. Cavalier King Charles

The Great Universal Studios Hollywood Scavenger Hunt

44. ★★ On the advertisement for McCutchen Family Farm, which of these is *not* one of the activities offered?
    a. Fleece you own wool
    b. Churn you own butter
    c. Make your own broom
    d. Pet the goats

45. ★ On the notice for upcoming events in central park, which event takes place on Saturday 11th, 11 am?
    a. Jazz concert
    b. Pet costume parade
    c. 5K fun run
    d. Outdoor movie *"Despicable Me 3"*

> **Did you know?**
> Watch the blinds outside the windows in the lobby. You will see Chloe the cat and Gidget the dog interact in the windows as you walk by.

> **Did you know?**
> Peek in the mail slots as you walk down the hallway and you will see what the pets are doing while their owners are away.

46. ★ When you enter the kitchen area, you will find a bowl of fruit on the counter. Which of these is *not* one of the types of fruit you see?
    a. Grapes
    b. Bananas
    c. Apples
    d. Oranges

> **Did you know?**
>
> As you walk down the hall between the room, look up at the air vent. You will see Norman the hamster wandering through the air ducts and chat with the guests working their way through the apartments.

47. ★★ As you enter the dining room at the top of the stairs, you will find framed posters for the New York Central Park Jazz Festival. What type of instrument is featured in the Illumination Mac Guff Orchestra?
    a. Tambourine
    b. Ukulele
    c. Kazoo
    d. Trombone

48. ★ Find the chalkboard in the kitchen area with the to do list. What sort of sports game is taking place that night?
    a. Hockey
    b. Baseball
    c. Soccer
    d. Football

49. ★ As you enter the child's bedroom, what color is the car sitting atop the wooden track?
    a. Red
    b. Blue
    c. Green
    d. Yellow

50. ★★ If you look at the books in the bookshelves, find and finish this title, "*The Saddest _____.*"
    a. Puppy
    b. Bunny
    c. Sandwich
    d. Princess

> **Did you know?**
>
> The wooden blocks sitting on the headboard spell out Liam. This is the name of the son Katie and Chuck have in Secret Life of Pets II.

The Great Universal Studios Hollywood Scavenger Hunt

51. ★ In the child's bedroom, you will see Norman the hamster in the air vent once again. What is his new fluffy new friend made from?
    a. Pet hair
    b. Cloth
    c. Dust
    d. Plastic

> **Did you know?**
> When you enter the living room area, this is a wonderful picture opportunity with the star of Secret Life of Pets, Max and Duke.

52. ★ When you enter the next room, watch the television screen and listen to Pops educate the puppies. Which of these is not one of the four food groups Princess mentions to Pops?
    a. Dry food
    b. Wet food
    c. Treats
    d. Floor food

53. ★★ As Pops talks about poop you will see one of the puppies pooping in the fish bowl. What sort of decoration does the fish hide inside?
    a. Treasure chest
    b. Castle
    c. Ship
    d. Octopus

54. ★★ What item does Pops tell you is worth your dignity at the end of his lesson?
    a. Table scraps
    b. Belly rubs
    c. New toys
    d. Sleeping on the bed

55. ★ As you enter the bedroom where Snowball is talking to the guests in the queue, he will refer to the map of the city, what color are the squiggles on the paper he refers to?
    a. Red
    b. Blue
    c. Black
    d. Orange

> **Did you know?**
> On the dresser is a clock in the shape of a Minion from *Despicable Me*. Illumination Entertainment produced both *Secret Life of Pets* and the *Despicable Me* movies.

56. ★ What color are the high-top sneakers next to the bed in the pink bedroom you pass through?
    a. Pink
    b. Green
    c. Yellow
    d. Red

> **Did you know?**
> The ride vehicle you step into is a cardboard box to transport you to the adoption center. Read some of the markings on the boxes used to keep the puppies in during your ride.

57. ★ As you enter your ride vehicle, notice a cardboard box sitting atop the refrigerator box. What words have been written on the side of the small box?
    a. Kitchen towels
    b. Bathroom
    c. Toys and games
    d. Bedroom linens

> **Did you know?**
> Look in the window of Village Electronics and you will see yourself as an adorable puppy.

58. ★★ Read the advertisements in the window of Katner's Deli, which item is on sale for $5.99?
    a. Corned beef on wheat
    b. Liverwurst on white
    c. Pastrami on rye
    d. Bratwurst on Kaiser

The Great Universal Studios Hollywood Scavenger Hunt

59. ★ According to the sign on the Weiner Kingdom cart, how long will the attendant be gone?
    a.   Five minutes
    b.   Ten minutes
    c.   Fifteen minutes
    d.   Thirty minutes
60. ★★★ In the window of Bleecker Books, you will find *Mr. Pokey's Great Zoo Escape*. What kind of animal is on the cover of this book?
    a.   Sloth
    b.   Turtle
    c.   Snail
    d.   Puppy
61. ★★★ What is the name of the author of Men are Cats and Women are Dogs in the window of Bleecker Books?
    a.   Dr. Chris Renaud
    b.   Dr. Frances Storey
    c.   Dr. Theodora Carlton
    d.   Dr. Lynne Dunn

> **Did you know?**
> As you enter the Pets Store, you will find a display of Minion shaped backpacks to the right on the lowest shelf.

62. ★★ On the shelves to the left of your ride vehicle, you will find several packages of Dog Biscuits. How many tasty bites are in this container?
    a.   Twenty-five
    b.   Twenty
    c.   Thirty-five
    d.   Fifty-five
63. ★★ What is the name of the automatic cat washing station you see Chloe getting groomed inside?
    a.   Wash-O-Matic
    b.   Pet-O-Matic
    c.   Scrub-O-Matic
    d.   Cat-O-Matic
64. ★★ When you arrive at the party, which pet has their foot stuck in a cupcake?
    a.   Gidget
    b.   Chloe
    c.   Norman
    d.   Daisy

65. ★ As you turn the corner from Secret Life of Pets: Off the Leash entrance, continue exploring and you will find a blue door at number 1481. This is the consulate of what fictional country?
    a. Freedonia
    b. Genovia
    c. Florin
    d. Lilliput

66. ★★★ At the corner you will find Village Bikes. As you read the notices on the door, what day of the week is the bike night scheduled?
    a. Saturday
    b. Friday
    c. Sunday
    d. Tuesday

67. ★★ Find the notice for the sidewalk sale going on this weekend. What is the name of the thrift store putting on this sale?
    a. Arthur's
    b. Judson's
    c. Troy's
    d. Bruno's

68. ★ Find the sign for Otto's Toys painted on the brick wall. What color is the Teddy bear on this sign?
    a. Yellow
    b. Red
    c. Purple
    d. White

69. ★★ Look in the window of Otto's Toys and find the display of colorful alphabet blocks stacked in the wooden frame. Which of these letters is *not* included on the display?
    a. Q
    b. M
    c. A
    d. X

70. ★ Find the pink stuffed pig in the window of Otto's Toys. What sort of hat does this toy wear on its head?
    a. Tiara
    b. Cowboy hat
    c. Bonnet
    d. Baseball cap

71. ★ Find the skateboard in the window of Otto's Toys. What color is this skateboard?
    a. Red
    b. Blue
    c. Green
    d. Black

The Great Universal Studios Hollywood Scavenger Hunt

72. ★ Find the stack of wooden alphabet blocks in the shape of a pyramid. What letter is on the block with the train?
    a. T   c. D
    b. C   d. J
73. ★★ What color is the car in the garage of the wooden doll house at Otto's Toys?
    a. Green   c. Red
    b. Yellow   d. Purple
74. ★★ Find the Palace Deli and Market on Pet's Place. If you look at the second story there is a sign in the window for Miss Kayte Elise's. What sort of lessons does she offer?
    a. Dancing   c. Music
    b. Sewing   d. Judo

Paris Street

From the Champs Elysees to Notre Dame, find romance on the streets of Paris. Buy your flowers from the charming street vendors and sit in a café while you sip an espresso. After the sun goes down, spend your evening at the famous Moulin Rouge all here on Paris Street.

> **Did you know?**
> This area of Universal Studios upper lot is fashioned after Paris in 1930. Look around at the shops and signs to bring you back to Europe during this era.

75. ✯✯ If you walk down Paris street, you will find a bill for the Moulin Rouge on the signpost. According to this sign, finish the following, "Les ____ Doriss Girls."
    a. 20   c. 40
    b. 30   d. 50

76. ✯✯✯ If you read the map for the metro lines attached to the signpost, which of these is at the end of the blue line?
    a. Balard   c. Orleans
    b. Vanves   d. Invalides

The Great Universal Studios Hollywood Scavenger Hunt

77. ★ Look across the street at the sign for Madam Mousseau. Which of these items does this shop sell?
    a. Hats
    b. Shoes
    c. Glasses
    d. Perfume
78. ★ Find the shop Le Chapeau Royal, in what year was this shop established?
    a. 1852
    b. 1862
    c. 1962
    d. 1586
79. ★★★ You will find a sign in the door of Le Chapeau Royal that reads, "Defense de fumer". What is the translation of this sign in English?
    a. Out to lunch
    b. Closed
    c. No smoking
    d. Help wanted
80. ★★ Find the small open box with the label Starfire written on it in the window. What does this box contain?
    a. A ring
    b. Cufflinks
    c. A pocket knife
    d. A lighter
81. ★ Walk a little further down the street and you will find the entrance to a courtyard. According to the sign, what is this courtyard name?
    a. De La Universale
    b. De La Parisian
    c. De La Laemmle
    d. De La Fontaine
82. ★★ As you step into the courtyard, what is the name of the hotel on your right?
    a. Lugosi
    b. Casanova
    c. Laemmle
    d. Valentino
83. ★★ How much is a double Deux Lits room at the hotel within the courtyard?
    a. One hundred
    b. Seven hundred fifty
    c. Seven hundred
    d. Five hundred

Despicable Me: Minion Mayhem

Join Gru and his girls as they celebrate together with the minions in Despicable Me: Minion Mayhem. Visit Gru's home and take a peek how they live before beginning your minion training. Do you have what it takes to become one of Gru's minions?

> **Did you know?**
>
> As you stand in front of the entrance to the Despicable Me: Minion Mayhem attraction, you will notice you are standing before Gru's house from the movie of the same name. This façade is complete with Gru's car. Just next door is Miss Hattie's home for girls where Gru adopts Margo Edith and Agnes.

84. ★ In what year was Miss Hattie's home for girls founded according to the plaque you see near the door?
    - a. 1966
    - b. 1976
    - c. 1986
    - d. 1906

The Great Universal Studios Hollywood Scavenger Hunt

> **Did you know?**
> Along the row of houses near the entrance to Gru's home, you will find doorbells for each house. Ring the door bells and listen for the neighbors to answer the doorbell.

85. ★★ As you enter the front door of Gru's house, you will see a wanted poster in the foyer. The governor from which state proclaimed this wanted man?
    a. Montana
    b. Mississippi
    c. Missouri
    d. Michigan

86. ★★ Look closely for the newspaper with the headline "Gru! Villain of the year". How many votes were cast for the win?
    a. Two Million
    b. Two Thousand
    c. Two votes
    d. Two Billion

87. ★★ Read the newspaper with the headline "What will he do next". What does the paper read beneath the picture on the front page?
    a. Sexiest man of the year
    b. He's not just a pretty face
    c. A face only a mother could love
    d. Can plastic surgery be far off?

88. ★★★ What is the title of the frog chart you see next to the newspapers on the wall?
    a. Frog legs menu
    b. Frogs from around the world
    c. Poison fart frogs
    d. Poison dart frogs

> **Did you know?**
>
> As you enter the first room of Gru's house, look at the shelves around you. You will find the helmet Gru made from a cardboard box, the macaroni prototype of his rocket and his original drawing of the rocket he showed his mother is the first *Despicable Me* movie.

89. ★★ As you read Gru's family tree, what is the name of the husband at the top of the chart?
    a. Leopold
    b. François
    c. Gru
    d. Lawrence

90. ★★ What is Gru's given name according to this chart?
    a. Gru
    b. Theodore
    c. Felonius
    d. Felton

91. ★★ As you look around the room, which of these is *not* one of the animals mounted on the wall?
    a. Bird
    b. Lion
    c. Mouse
    d. Cat

92. ★ As Gru and the girls begin the introduction to Minion training, what animal is Gru's couch made from?
    a. Rhinoceros
    b. Alligator
    c. Polar Bear
    d. Whale

93. ★ What object does Edith hold up and call her evil clown?
    a. Unicorn
    b. Teddy bear
    c. Fashion doll
    d. Sock puppet

94. ★ How long will the written exam take to complete according to Gru?
    a. Three days
    b. Three hours
    c. Three weeks
    d. Three minutes

The Great Universal Studios Hollywood Scavenger Hunt

95. ★ The goggles you have will last five times longer than what?
    a. A package of Twinkies
    b. Cockroaches
    c. Cher
    d. The person wearing them

96. ★★ As the minion eats Jalapeno dip, what is in the framed picture in the background?
    a. A fork
    b. Gru's portrait
    c. Flower vase
    d. Minions

97. ★★ As Gru begins your interview, you will see a minion come to him with blue prints. When the minion hands Gru the plans, what does he tell him they need more of?
    a. Gun powder
    b. Freeze rays
    c. Explosions
    d. Dynamite

98. ★★★ What is the scent of the fart gun Gru shoots at you in the pre-boarding room?
    a. Fart
    b. Pineapple
    c. Banana
    d. Rotten fruit

99. ★★ As you begin minion training, you will jump over what object in the obstacle course?
    a. A banana
    b. A cactus
    c. A bomb
    d. A fart gun

100. ★★ As you continue running the obstacle course, what are you and the other minions being hit with?
    a. Swings
    b. Hammer
    c. Fly swatter
    d. Glove

101. ★ What color is the bow on Gru's present from the girls?
    a. Yellow
    b. Red
    c. Blue
    d. Green

102. ★ What is unusual about the recycle area of Gru's lab?
    a. Under water
    b. It's on the moon
    c. High frequency
    d. Anti-gravity

103. ✶ What is inside the present from Agnes to Gru for their anniversary?
    a.   Minion doll
    b.   Unicorn toy
    c.   Gru doll
    d.   Sleepy kitty book

> ### Did you know?
> Stop for a dance party on the way out of Despicable Me: Minion Mayhem. The music is pumpin' so get your groove on and see yourself on the big screen.

104. ✶✶ As you exit Despicable Me: Minion Mayhem, you will see a mural to your left. How many minions do you see on the Ferris wheel?
    a.   Four
    b.   Five
    c.   Seven
    d.   Fifteen

105. ✶ How many teeth does the green monster have on the mural to your left?
    a.   Five
    b.   Six
    c.   Two
    d.   Seven

> ### Did you know?
> If you are waiting for the cash register within the Despicable Me shop, look down at your feet. The wait here sign is a pile of banana peels left by the minions.

Super Silly Fun Land

> **Did you know?**
> As you exit the store, you will find Stuart, Bob and Dave in the minion mobile dressed for a day of shopping. Be sure to pose for a picture with these three famous minions before they speed away.

106. ★★ As you walk around Super Silly Fun Land, what color is the paint the minions are using outside?
 a. Pink c. Blue
 b. Yellow d. Green

> **Did you know?**
> If look at the mural on the outside of the building, you will find a small Gru riding the roller coaster.

107. ★ What animal shape does the drinking fountain in Super Silly Fun Land resemble?
 a. Shark c. Squid
 b. Frog d. Fish

> **Did you know?**
> As you play in Super Silly Fun Land you will find two minions roasting a hot dog and a marshmallow over a volcano. If you look inside the volcano, you will see minion eyes looking back out at you.

108. ★★ If you look high above your head you will find the minions eating their lunch on a scaffold on the front of the building. How many minions do you see?
    a. Six
    b. Five
    c. Thirty-two
    d. Seven

109. ★★ As you wander through the wet zone, you will find a minion with an inner tube around his waist. What animal is on the inner tube?
    a. A frog
    b. A duck
    c. A bunny
    d. An alligator

> **Did you know?**
> As you exit Super Silly Fun Land and Despicable Me: Minion Mayhem, look at the two minions standing sentry at the gates. Notice they are holding fart guns to keep away unwanted characters.

DreamWorks™ Theater Featuring Kung Fu Panda

110. ★ As you approach the DreamWorks™ Theater, which DreamWorks™ character is working in the ticket booth at the entrance?
    a. The three pigs
    b. Donkey
    c. Pinocchio
    d. Shrek

> **Did you know?**
> Listen to Pinocchio as he sleeps and you will hear him talk to the different characters throughout Universal Studios theme park in his dreams.

111. ★★★ As you walk down the side of the DreamWorks™ theater, you will see several movie posters from various DreamWorks™ creations. Which of these is *not* one of the DreamWorks™ animated films you see?
    a. *Dinosaur*
    b. *Trolls*
    c. *Home*
    d. *The Croods*

112. ★★★ Before entering the DreamWorks™ Theater, you will walk through an archway with a metal decoration. If you look carefully, you will see silhouettes of several characters. Which character is at the bottom on the left side?
   a. Shrek
   b. Marty
   c. Toothless
   d. Po

113. ★★ As you enter the lobby of the DreamWorks™ theater, stop for a moment to look at the various awards in the glass case. Which DreamWorks™ film won the 2008 People's Choice Award™ for Favorite Family Movie?
   a. *Shrek the Third*
   b. *Shrek*
   c. *Kung Fu Panda*
   d. *Madagascar 2 Escape 2 Africa*

114. ★★ Find the 2014 Annie Award™ for Best Animated Feature. Which of the following DreamWorks™ films won this award?
   a. *Megamind*
   b. *How to Train your Dragon*
   c. *Trolls*
   d. *Madagascar*

115. ★★★ As you continue your search through the many awards, you will find the Golden Globe™ award between the statues of Po and Alex. Which film won the 2014 Golden Globe™ for Best Animated Feature Film?
   a. *How to Train your Dragon*
   b. *Madagascar 3: Europe's Most Wanted*
   c. *How to Train your Dragon 2*
   d. *Penguins of Madagascar*

116. ★★★ Which of the following won the 2001 Critic's Choice Award™ for Best Animated Feature?
   a. *The Road to El Dorado*
   b. *Joseph: King of Dreams*
   c. *Shark Tale*
   d. *Shrek*

The Great Universal Studios Hollywood Scavenger Hunt

> **Did you know?**
> Above the awards, you will find a small magic mirror. This mirror is a nod to the Shrek 4D attraction that was housed in this theater staring in 2003 and closing in 2017 to make room for the DreamWorks™ theater.

117. ★★★ As the pre-show begins, you see the penguins from Madagascar. Which of these penguins shuts off the lights in the lobby?
     a. Skipper
     b. Rico
     c. Mort
     d. Kowalski
118. ★★★ What drink does Skipper ask for after the lights go out in the lobby?
     a. Macchiato
     b. Venti decaf
     c. Frappuccino
     d. Vanilla shake
119. ★ What color is the balloon Poppy flies in on?
     a. Red
     b. Blue
     c. White
     d. Yellow
120. ★★ As Po talks about the artifacts in the glass, who is the owner of the helmet he points to first?
     a. Kai the Collector
     b. Tai Lung
     c. Thundering Rhino
     d. Master Shifu
121. ★★ What is the correct name of the sword Po shows you within the case?
     a. Sword of Pandas
     b. Sword of Tai Lung
     c. Sword of Ninja's
     d. Sword of Heroes
122. ★★ How does Mr. Ping know Po has been asked to deliver something to the Emperor?
     a. The Emperor told him
     b. He is Psychic
     c. He read his mail
     d. Master Shifu told him

123. ★★ Finish this line, Mr. Ping tells Po he is to deliver the "Liquid of _____" to the Emperor.
    a. Ultimate power
    b. The kings
    c. The ages
    d. The dynasty
124. ★★ When Po tells Poppy he needs bigger warriors, what does she suggest they do?
    a. Have a surprise party
    b. Have a tea party
    c. Go to Disneyland
    d. Watch television
125. ★★★ Before the doors to the theater open, Po comes back to urge you to hurry before who changes their mind?
    a. Master Shifu
    b. Kang
    c. The Emperor
    d. Oogway
126. ★★★ Which of these DreamWorks characters was *not* seen during the pre-show in the lobby?
    a. Marty the Zebra
    b. Alex the lion
    c. Poppy
    d. Shrek

> **Did you know?**
> The DreamWorks™ logo at the top of the doorway animates to let you into the theater. This logo was designed by none other than Stephen Spielberg himself.

127. ★★ Which DreamWorks™ character advises you to push and shove your way to your seat in the theater?
    a. Kang
    b. Gingy
    c. Marty
    d. Skipper
128. ★★ When you hear Gingy over the speakers, he says he is so excited he could burst his what?
    a. Frosting
    b. Bowtie
    c. Gumdrop buttons
    d. Candy cane

129. ★★ As you being your journey to deliver the liquid of ultimate power to the Emperor, which character does Mr. Ping call butter fingers?
    a. Po
    b. Master Shifu
    c. Oogway
    d. Tai Lung

130. ★ As you ride the white water, Po says the river looks like it just ends up ahead. What reason does Master Shifu give to the river ending?
    a. River bank
    b. Cave
    c. They run out of water
    d. Waterfall

131. ★ As you land on the wooden scaffolding, what type of animals are running out of your way as you pass?
    a. Bunnies
    b. Wolves
    c. Dogs
    d. Pandas

> **Did you know?**
>
> As you enter the Kang territory, watch the walls around you. The fire flies are floating around the entire theater. Continue looking around you as your adventure continues and you will see flaming arrows pierce the walls.

132. ★★ What sort of dreaded fiends are Kang's gang of wolves?
    a. River warriors
    b. River pirates
    c. River raiders
    d. River dogs

133. ★ As you arrive at the palace, how many musicians do you see playing on the steps?
    a. Five
    b. Eight
    c. Three
    d. Two

134. ★★ When Kang arrives at the Emperor's palace, where does he say he will defeat Po?
    a. On the river bank
    b. At the palace
    c. In his lair
    d. In the spirit realm

135. ★★★ As Po fights Kang, Kang forces Po to choose between the liquid of ultimate power and who?
    a. Master Shifu
    b. The Emperor
    c. Himself
    d. Ping
136. ★★ As Po arrives back at the palace, what does the emperor say was his special delivery?
    a. Po
    b. The liquid of ultimate power
    c. Kang
    d. The boat
137. ★★ What was contained in the bottle they delivered to the palace?
    a. Liquid of ultimate power
    b. Ping's secret ingredient hot sauce
    c. River water
    d. Royal hot sauce
138. ★★ After Po drinks the contents of the bottle, what does the emperor say his tongue is as formidable as?
    a. His weight
    b. His appetite
    c. His kung fu
    d. His family

> ### Did you know?
> As you exit the DreamWorks™ theater listen and you will hear your favorite characters talking to you on your way down the path. See how many different character voices you can hear.

The Great Universal Studios Hollywood Scavenger Hunt

Did you know?

Across the road from the DreamWorks™ theater you will find an area with a decorative backdrop. Some of your favorite DreamWorks™ characters can be found in this area for pictures and autograph signing. Keep an eye out for Shrek, Fiona and your favorite Trolls.

Next to the DreamWorks™ theater, you will find a kiosk with travel posters. Your travel agent, Donkey can be found in this area to chat with guests and get pictures.

Wizarding World of Harry Potter

As you enter the magical mystical world of Harry, Hermione and Ron, you will explore the well-known shops and attractions that bring you right to the heart of the Harry Potter books. Become a wizard yourself when you don your robes, hold your wand and transport yourself to a world where anything is possible.

> ### Did you know?
> Throughout Hogsmeade there are special interactive surprises. For those that have the interactive wand, get ready to cast some spells of your own.

1. ✯✯✯ As you enter Hogsmeade you will see the Hogwarts Express to your right. Take a look at the timetable on the station, what holiday is included with the Saturday/Sunday grid?

The Great Universal Studios Hollywood Scavenger Hunt

    a.   Christmas   c.   Boxing day
    b.   Halloween   d.   Easter

2. ✯✯✯ As you read the time table, what is the first fare from Cardiff to Kingly Langley on Tuesday?
    a. 50.00   c. 69.45
    b. 62.50   d. 45.69
3. ✯✯✯ According to the Hogsmeade timetable, what is the date of registration of this document?
    a. 24 February   c. 30 November
    b. 24 December   d. 31 December

Zonko's Trick's and Jokes

4. ✯✯ As you stand outside Zonko's Tricks and Jokes, take a look at the window display. What number do the robots have stamped on their bodies?
    a. 5753   c. 3735
    b. 7573   d. 5357
5. ✯ What kind of animal is riding on the bike in the front window display?
    a. Chicken   c. Dog
    b. Duck   d. Pike
6. ✯✯ What kind of eye wear does the man in the window of Zonko's wear?
    a. Monocle   c. Bifocals
    b. Opera glasses d. Opera glasses

Did you know?

As you look in the window of Zonko's, watch the display for Puking Pastilles. The poor display keeps filling the bucket continuously throughout the day.

> **Did you know?**
> If you watch the Wizard's chess board in the window, watch carefully and you will see the chess pieces move on their own to destroy their opponent.

7. ★ As you enter Zonko's, look at the rafters above your head. What insect do you find?
   a. Honey Bees
   b. Flies
   c. Butterflies
   d. Mosquitos
8. ★★ As you look at the rafters above you, which of these is *not* one of the animal heads you see?
   a. Elephant
   b. Donkey
   c. Buffalo
   d. Zebra
9. ★ Find the statue of the dog wearing a party hat, what does he hold in his mouth?
   a. Bone
   b. Yoyo
   c. Duck
   d. Boomerang

Honeydukes

10. ★★ As you look at the window of Honeydukes, how many skeletons do you see on the staircases?
    a. Fifteen
    b. Twenty
    c. Twenty-five
    d. Thirty

> **Did you know?**
> Watch the skeleton in the Eyeball Bonanza machine in the window of Honeydukes. When he raises his hat to reveals a crow that reaches down to pluck out his eye. Watch closely as his eye will appear in the dispenser below ready for you to take.

The Great Universal Studios Hollywood Scavenger Hunt

11. ★★★ As you enter Honeydukes, how many pink lollypops line the walls around this shop?
    a. Twenty-four
    b. Thirty-four
    c. Fourteen
    d. Forty-four
12. ★ Read the menu for Honeydukes behind the counter, which of these is the third pastry down written in green?
    a. Fudge
    b. Pumpkin Pasties
    c. Pretzel Wands
    d. Pumpkin cakes
13. ★★★ As you exit Honeydukes, take a walk around this building to a hidden alley. If you look in the window behind Honeydukes, how many red snake heads do you find in and around the glass jar display?
    a. Six
    b. Twenty-three
    c. Sixty-one
    d. Sixteen

The Three Broomsticks

> **Did you know?**
> As you enter The Three Broomsticks, look around you at the walls. Notice fairies and elves appearing in shadows around you throughout the room.

14. ★★★ Throughout the Three Broomsticks you will find antlers displayed. How many total antlers are there displayed within this restaurant?
    a. Twenty-six
    b. Thirty-six
    c. Sixteen
    d. Sixty-three

Catherine F. Olen

Hog's Head

15. ★★ Next door to the Three Broomsticks is the Hogs Head pub. As you enter this establishment find the round chalk board. Which of these is *not* one of the items brought from around the world?
    a. Meat
    b. Vegetables
    c. Ale
    d. Sauces
16. ★★ Which one of these items is on the chalk board for yesterday's specials?
    a. Steak and Kidney pudding
    b. Steak and Kidney Pie
    c. Kipper Pudding
    d. Kipper Pie
17. ★★ As you look around this room, read the sign directing you how to leave after what hour?
    a. The witching hour
    b. Closing time
    c. Midnight
    d. Morning

> **Did you know?**
> Notice the hogs head behind the bar. Watch carefully as the mounted head moves side to side and snorts his displeasure at the patrons.

18. ★ How many shrunken heads do you find behind the bar?
    a. Three
    b. Four
    c. Five
    d. One
19. ★ What does the warning sign behind the bar remind you not to lose?
    a. Your wallet
    b. Your head
    c. Your wand
    d. Your lunch

The Great Universal Studios Hollywood Scavenger Hunt

> ### Did you know?
> Walk towards the staircase to the left of the bar. If you listen carefully, you will hear the elves working hard to wait on the guests on the second floor.

20. ★ What does the label on the container of eggs read sitting behind the bar at the Hogs Head pub?
    a. Doxy eggs
    b. b Dragon eggs
    c. Pickled eggs
    d. Whiskey eggs
21. ★★★ Read the labels on the bottles behind the bar, what type of whiskey is served from the bottle with the red label and the spigot?
    a. Black dog whiskey
    b. Red kitten whiskey
    c. Green dragon whiskey
    d. White rat whiskey
22. ★★★ White Rat Whisky comes from the cellar of warlocks of what city?
    a. Alexandria
    b. Zanzibar
    c. Hogsmeade
    d. Tanzania
23. ★★★ If you read the blue label on the bottle to the left of Blishen's Fire Whiskey, how many years was this liquor aged in copper cauldrons?
    a. Fifteen
    b. Twenty-one
    c. Nineteen
    d. Eighteen

> ### Did you know?
> As you walk down the street of Hogsmeade, stop in front of Dogweed and Deathcap. Notice the ear muffs laying in the window. Be sure to don these Earmuff before replanting the mandrake you see in the window.

24. ★★★ Stop in front of the window of Madam Puddifoot's. How many bright pink cakes with whipped cream do you see?
    a. Twelve
    b. Twenty-three
    c. Seventeen
    d. Seventy-one
25. ★★★ As you peek in the right window of Madam Puddifoot's, among the teacups how many teaspoons can you find?
    a. Nine
    b. Twelve
    c. Thirty-two
    d. Four

> ### Did you know?
> If you are running low on funds during your visit to Hogsmeade, stop at the Gringotts™ ATM in the alley to the left of Ollivanders.

26. ★★★ Notice the windows above the conveniences marked J. Pippins. If you read the label on the bottle with the green potion, what does it contain?
    a. Gilly weed
    b. Silver Weed
    c. Pumpkin extract
    d. Mandrake saliva

Ollivanders

27. ★ As you stand in front of Ollivanders, in what year was this wand shop established?
    a. 832 BC
    b. 382 BC
    c. 832 AD
    d. 382 AD
28. ★★ As you watch the wand fitting, how is the wizard fitted for their wand?
    a. The wand chooses the wizard
    b. By length
    c. The wizard chooses the wand
    d. Go to the gift shop

The Great Universal Studios Hollywood Scavenger Hunt

> **Did you know?**
> As you step outside and back to the main street, find the water trough by the conveniences. Notice the water is frozen over. This is designed in keeping with the time of year. Look around at the snow on the rooftops and icicles on the eaves. Feels like it is time to bundles up in your Hogwarts™ robe and scarf.

Owl Post™

29. ✯✯✯ As you look in the front window of the Owl Post™, see the mail in the mailboxes. What number is on the Hogwarts™ ticket in box five hundred sixty?
    a. Two hundred seventy-five
    b. Two hundred fifty-seven
    c. One thousand nine hundred one
    d. Seven hundred fifty-two

30. ✯✯ On the side of the Owl Post you will find packages in the window. Watch as a howler appears between the packages. What did you go to Hogsmeade without according to the howler?
    a. Permission form
    b. Enchantment
    c. Broom
    d. Wand

31. ✯✯ According to the howler, what kind of ball did you practice Quidditch with?
    a. Golden Snitch
    b. Golden
    c. Crystal
    d. Rubber

32. ✯✯ As you enter the Owl Post, look around at the hundreds of packages in this room. Look in the window to your right, what musical instrument is wrapped for shipping?
    a. Guitar
    b. Flute
    c. Violin
    d. Piano

33. ★★★ As you look at the packages above the window with the tear in the blind, what wizarding equipment is wrapped in this area?
    a. Spell book
    b. Broom
    c. Wand
    d. Cauldron

> ### Did you know?
> As you look around the Owl Post, you will see several owls on their perches ready to fly to their destinations. Watch as their heads turn and notice the droppings on their perches.

Dervish and Banges

34. ★ As you walk into the store behind the Owl Post, notice the book in the cage. What does the warning sign above the cage read, "Danger, Book may _____?"
    a. Snap
    b. Bite
    c. Sting
    d. Escape
35. ★★ Read the closing procedure hanging behind the counter, what does number seven tell you to do?
    a. Extinguish the lights
    b. Check the lock on the book cage
    c. Exit the store
    d. Cast a security spell
36. ★★★ Look very carefully at the inventory on the second floor. Find the glass jugs, what do they contain?
    a. Horklump juice
    b. Pumpkin juice
    c. Gilly water
    d. Butter beer

The Great Universal Studios Hollywood Scavenger Hunt

> **Did you know?**
> Watch the brooms tied up above your head. See how they sway back and forth waiting for their riders to come back to get them.

37. ★ Step outside Dervish and Banges and find the window display. What sort of broom is advertised?
    a. Firebolt
    b. Nimbus 2001
    c. Nimbus 2000
    d. Cumulus 2000
38. ★★ Find the bottle with the black label in the window. What is contained in this bottle?
    a. Porcuquils
    b. Owl juice
    c. Bluebird potion
    d. Dragon blood
39. ★★★ In the window of Dervish and Banges you will find a large frame with wooden beads attached. What is the name of this counting device?
    a. Calculator
    b. Abacus
    c. Timer
    d. Bead painter

> **Did you know?**
> Within the window of Dervish and Banges you will find a scale model of Hogwarts™ School of Witchcraft and Wizardry.

40. ★★ Head back to the window of the Owl Post with the howler that appears. What did you go over for hours to prepare for according to the howler you receive?
    a. Potions
    b. Transfiguration
    c. Herbology
    d. Defense against the dark arts O.W.L.S.

41. ★★ What is the reason your presents are going back to Hogsmeade according to the howler?
    a. Forgot to buy gifts for your family
    b. Didn't come home for the holiday
    c. Received low marks in your classes
    d. Broke your broomstick

Gladrags Wizardwear

42. ★★ Look in the window of Gladrags Wizardwear and you will see a measuring tape in the shape of what animal?
    a. A turkey
    b. A cat
    c. A dog
    d. An owl
43. ★ On the sign for Gladrags Wizardwear, which of these cities is *not* a location for Gladrags?
    a. London
    b. Hogsmeade
    c. Rome
    d. Paris
44. ★ Step inside Gladrags Wizardwear and look up at the second floor. What do they offer while you wait?
    a. Tailoring
    b. Hemming
    c. Repairs
    d. Robes

> ### Did you know?
> If you look at the second floor of Gladrags, you will notice several dresses on mannequins. These are original costumes worn by the actresses from the Harry Potter series of movies.

Tomes and Scrolls Specialist Bookshop

45. ★ In what year was Tomes and Scrolls Specialist Bookshop established?
    a. 1678
    b. 1768
    c. 1968
    d. 1876

The Great Universal Studios Hollywood Scavenger Hunt

46. ★★ As you look in the window of Tomes and Scrolls, notice several books by famed wizard Gilderoy Lockhart. Which of these titles is *not* in the window?
    a. *Meandering with Mummies*
    b. *Year with a Yeti*
    c. *Travels with Trolls*
    d. *Break with a Banshee*

> **Did you know?**
> As you read the titles of Gilderoy Lockhart's books, you will find one entitled, *Who Am I?* This book is a reference to the second Harry Potter book, *The Chamber of Secrets* where Lockhart loses his memory after his spell backfires on him.

47. ★★ Continue your exploration of Hogsmeade and you will find a street behind Gladrags Wizardwear. Stand before the window of The Magic Neep. Which of these signs is *not* in the window?
    a. Neeps
    b. Eggs
    c. Squash
    d. Fruit

48. ★ Next to the Magic Neep you will find a stack of cauldrons, how many cauldrons do you count in this stack?
    a. Eight
    b. Fifteen
    c. Ten
    d. Seventeen

Flight of the Hippogriff™

49. ★ As you walk through the line for Flight of the Hippogriff, what sort of vegetable does Hagrid grow in his garden?
    a. Watermelon
    b. Corn
    c. Green beans
    d. Pumpkin

> ### Did you know?
> As you walk through Hagrid's garden, notice his scarecrow is wearing a Hogwarts robe.

50. ★★★ Listen carefully as you approach Hagrid's shack. What warning do you hear him giving?
    a. The forest is forbidden to all students
    b. The spiders will kill you
    c. Do not mess with Mr. Filch
    d. Draco Malfoy is going to cause you trouble

> ### Did you know?
> Listen carefully as you walk by Hagrid's hut, you can hear Fang barking at the strangers invading his house.

Bonus Question

51. ★★★ As you walk by Hagrid's, you will see his motorbike parked outside. Which Harry Potter character owned this bike before Hagrid?
    a. Lord Voldemort
    b. James Potter
    c. Sirius Black
    d. Albus Dumbledore

52. ★ As you walk by Hagrid's you will see a crate that once contained a baby dragon. Which breed of dragon was held in this crate?
    a. Romanian Longhorn
    b. Norwegian Ridgeback
    c. Hungarian Horntail
    d. Peruvian Vipertooth

The Great Universal Studios Hollywood Scavenger Hunt

Harry Potter and the Forbidden journey™

53. ★★ As you enter the dungeon of Hogwarts castle, one of the first things you see is the Mirror of Erised. What word is seen at the very top point of the mirror?
    a. Out
    b. Ub
    c. Ehru
    d. Erised

> ### Did you know?
> The Mirror of Erised shows the person looking into the mirror the deepest darkest desire of his heart. Did you notice the words around the mirror say, "I show not your face but your heart's desire" spelled backwards?

54. ★★★ Stop for a moment at the door for the potion's classroom, which Hogwarts student is being tutored as you listen through the door?
    a. Harry
    b. Ron
    c. Neville
    d. Draco

> ### Did you know?
> As you enter the Herbology area notice the small area to the right of the castle entrance with several kinds of plants. As you walk by, be sure to take notice of the baby mandrakes in the clay pots.

55. ★ As you enter the castle, notice the statue of the architect of Hogwarts castle standing to the right. What does he hold in his left hand?
    a. A scroll
    b. A castle
    c. A key
    d. A wand

56. ★★ Nearby you will see the glass hourglasses for the house points. As you look at the hourglasses, which house is winning?
    a. Hufflepuff
    b. Slytherin
    c. Ravenclaw
    d. Gryffindor

> **Did you know?**
> At the end of this hall you will see a large statue of a bird. This is the secret entrance to the office of Albus Dumbledore, headmaster of Hogwarts.

57. ★★ As you enter the portrait hall, you will see portraits of the four founders of Hogwarts. As they talk back and forth about Hagrid losing a Dragon, which building do they hope will not get burned down again?
    a. The chapel
    b. The owlery
    c. Hagrid's hut
    d. Herbology

58. ★★★ Salazar Slytherin speaks from his paintings saying this sounds like a clear violation of the warlock convention of what year?
    a. 1709
    b. 1907
    c. 1207
    d. 1509

59. ★★ Which of the four portraits detests muggles entering Hogwarts school?
    a. Godric Gryffindor
    b. Helga Hufflepuff
    c. Rowena Ravenclaw
    d. Salazar Slytherin

60. ★★ As you approach Dumbledore's office, he will greet you and talk about the students of Hogwarts. He says some have strayed where?
    a. The haunted forest
    b. The dark side
    c. The Death Eaters
    d. The village of Hogsmeade

The Great Universal Studios Hollywood Scavenger Hunt

61. ★ What is Tom Riddle known as these days according to Dumbledore?
    a. Tom Riddle
    b. Severus Snape
    c. Lord Voldemort
    d. Sirius Black
62. ★★ Dumbledore tells you there comes a time in everyone's life when they must make a choice between what is right and what?
    a. What is wrong
    b. What is evil
    c. What is lazy
    d. What is easy
63. ★★ How long will the hundreds of years of Hogwarts history be condensed down to according to Dumbledore?
    a. A few short hours
    b. A few short days
    c. A few short years
    d. A few short minutes

> ### Did you know?
> As you walk through the office of Albus Dumbledore, look closely and you will find the pensieve Harry Potter used to look at people's memories.

64. ★ How do Ron, Hermione and Harry enter the defense against the dark arts classroom?
    a. Walked in
    b. Flew in on brooms
    c. Waved their wands
    d. Cloak of invisibility
65. ★★ What does Hermione say to you about the history of Hogwarts?
    a. It's boring
    b. It's fascinating
    c. It's long
    d. It's light reading
66. ★★ What do Harry, Ron, and Hermione invite you to do?
    a. Go for a bite to eat
    b. See a play
    c. See a game of Quidditch
    d. Sneak into the dark forest

67. ★★ What happens in the classroom as the trio are chatting with you?
    a. It starts to rain
    b. Time goes backwards
    c. The sun comes out
    d. It starts snowing
68. ★★★ Stop to read the black board in the defense against the dark arts classroom. What do dementors force victims to do?
    a. Relive your childhood
    b. Relive your worst memories
    c. Believe you can't accomplish your dreams
    d. Make you forget your family
69. ★★ Continue reading the blackboard. To cast the Patronus charm, think of a single what?
    a. Happy memory
    b. Thing you like
    c. Happy little thought
    d. Person you want to help
70. ★ The skeleton of what creature hangs above you in the defense against the dark arts classroom?
    a. Unicorn
    b. Spider
    c. Dragon
    d. Owl
71. ★★★ As you walk the hallway between the defense against the dark arts classroom and the Gryffindor common room, stop for a moment to read the notices on the bulletin board. Which student posted the lost cauldron notice on this bulletin board?
    a. George Weasley
    b. Luna Lovegood
    c. Tom Riddle
    d. Peter Jones
72. ★★★ Which two houses are meeting in the Great Hall for wizard chess practice after dinner?
    a. Ravenclaw and Hufflepuff
    b. Hufflepuff and Gryffindor
    c. Slytherin and Ravenclaw
    d. Slytherin and Gryffindor

The Great Universal Studios Hollywood Scavenger Hunt

> **Did you know?**
> As you walk away from the defense against the dark arts classroom, stop for a moment at the painting of the woman who guards the Gryffindor common room. She will cheer for Gryffindor in the Quidditch match from time to time.

73. ✯✯ As you come to the sorting hat, you must be taller than what size to ride this attraction?
    a. Goblin
    b. Troll
    c. Pixie
    d. Dragon

74. ✯✯ The sorting hat advises you to put your belongings in lockers that are enchanted to protect from what?
    a. Dementor
    b. Death Eater
    c. Wizard
    d. Magic

75. ✯ Which student of Hogwarts creates the enchantment so your ride will fly?
    a. Harry
    b. Hermione
    c. Ron
    d. Neville

76. ✯ What does Hagrid hold up when he asks you if you've seen a dragon?
    a. A rope
    b. A dragon egg
    c. A wand
    d. A metal chain and collar

> **Did you know?**
> As the dragon is chasing you around the castle, did you notice the dragon claw marks along the roof just before he appears?

77. ★★ What does Hermione warn you to watch out for after she saves you from the spiders?
    a. The whoomphing willow
    b. The dementors
    c. The death eaters
    d. The quidditch pit
78. ★ After your daring escape from the dementors, where does Harry tell you to go?
    a. The tower
    b. The Gryffindor common room
    c. The great hall
    d. Dumbledore's office
79. ★★★ Which of these choices is *not* one of the challenges you faced on Harry Potter and the Forbidden Journey?
    a. Dementor
    b. Dragon
    c. Whoomphing Willow
    d. Lord Voldemort
80. ★★★ As you exit Harry Potter and the Forbidden Journey, you will arrive at Filch's Emporium of Confiscated Goods. As you look around at the items along the ceiling that Mr. Filch has taken from students of Hogwarts, what belonging of Harry Potter's do you find?
    a. His wand
    b. His Cloak of invisibility
    c. His glasses
    d. His owl

Did you know?

As you walk around Filch's Emporium of Confiscated Goods, look at the boxes that sit atop the shelves around the room. As you read the names written on the tags on the front of these boxes, you may notice some familiar names. Mr. Filch has confiscated personal belongings from some of your favorite Harry Potter characters.

Universal Studios Shows

Universal Studios would not be the phenomenon it is today without the live demonstrations of the special effects used in motion pictures. Since the beginnings of the theme park, guests have watch animal actors show off the training they receive for television and movies. The guests have been participants in special effects shows that have included flying in space, combatting oversized cats, creating foley sounds and escaping from giant beasts.

In the 1970's, guests could live their dream of becoming the Six Million Dollar Man by lifting a truck with one hand, flying through space on the S.S. Enterprise or having their limb severed by a horror villain.

The special effects did not stop there. Over the years, guests have gotten a glimpse behind the camera with stunt shows like The A Team, Miami Vice and the Water World Spectacular. You will not want to miss any of these shows during your stay at Universal Studios Hollywood.

Special Effects Show

Universal Studios has been on the cutting edge of special effects for over one hundred years. Get up close and personal with the experts as you go behind the magic of every aspect of movie making.

> ### Did you know?
> Get to this show early to get your chance to be selected as a volunteer for the next show. Depending on your talent, you could be selected as a Foley artist, an astronaut or even a scream queen.

1. ★★ As the Universal Studios Special Effects show begins, you will see an antique manufactured by the Pettibone brothers. What is the correct name of this invention?
    a. Magic lamp
    b. Magic lantern
    c. Magic projector
    d. Magic movies

The Great Universal Studios Hollywood Scavenger Hunt

2. ★★ As you watch the introduction to the Special Effect show, you will see several clips from the movies Universal Studios has produced. What does actor Samuel Jackson say in the scene from *Jurassic Park*?
   a. Hold on to your butts
   b. Hold on to your hats
   c. Buckle up and hold on
   d. Hold on, I'm not ready

3. ★★ In the scene from *Secret Life of Pets*, you see the fluffy white bunny carve a carrot into what shape?
   a. A lock
   b. A hat
   c. A key
   d. A boat

4. ★ According to your host, the film making process is to make the audience believe everything they see is _____.
   a. Magic
   b. Spectacular
   c. Larger than life
   d. Real

Bonus question:

5. ★★ As your hosts describe the use of practical effects, you see the introduction to the Universal classic film *The Mummy*. What famous actor portrayed the mummy in this film?
   a. Bela Lugosi
   b. Claude Raines
   c. Boris Karloff
   d. Robert Englund

6. ★ What Alfred Hitchcock classic is the backdrop for the demonstration of the glass matte process?
   a. *Psycho*
   b. *The Birds*
   c. *North by Northwest*
   d. *Dial M for Murder*

7. ★★ As the stunt team makes their amazing entrance, what reason does your host give why they did not get a similar entrance?
   a. It is too scary
   b. They are afraid of heights
   c. It is too flashy
   d. They are wearing nice pants

> ### Did you know?
> As you watch the fight scene performed by the stunt performers, listen carefully as the second bad guy gets thrown into the trash bin. You will hear the sound of a cat screeching from inside the dumpster.

8. ★★★ As you listen to the history of Jack Foley, which of these is *not* one of his professional credits listed by your host?
   a. Actor
   b. Director of silent films
   c. Stunt double
   d. Writer of Westerns

9. ★ How many years did Jack Foley work in sound stage ten on the Universal backlot?
   a. Over twenty
   b. Over forty
   c. Over thirty
   d. Over fifty

Bonus question:

10. ★★★ As you begin watching the introduction to the horror genre, you will see a scene from the original Universal Studios classic, *The Hunchback of Notre Dame*. What legendary actor played this iconic role?
    a. Bela Lugosi
    b. Lon Chaney
    c. Boris Karloff
    d. Claude Raines

The Great Universal Studios Hollywood Scavenger Hunt

11. ★ Your hosts will ask the audience what Alfred Hitchcock used for movie blood in the classic film, *Psycho*. Which of these is the correct answer?
    a. Chocolate syrup
    b. Red corn syrup
    c. Grenadine syrup
    d. Animal blood
12. ★★ On the stage you will see a variety of movie monster statues brought out to the center of the stage. What name do you see on the tombstone in front of the group of monsters on the left?
    a. Freddy Krueger
    b. Jason Voorhees
    c. Norman Bates
    d. Michael Meyers

Bonus question:

13. ★★★ As you watch the introduction for the fire stunt, you will see several scenes from films featuring fire stunts. You will see a young actress hiding from Michael Meyers in one scene, can you name this famous actress?
    a. Heather Langenkamp
    b. Janet Leigh
    c. Jamie Lee Curtis
    d. Jessica Lange

> ### Did you know?
> The fire stunt is a highly technical and dangerous stunt. The host urges the audience not to try this stunt at home. This is a solemn warning and should never be attempted by anyone without professional training or without specialized equipment as you are seeing on the stage.

Universal's Animal Actors

J oin the biggest stars in Hollywood as they show you what is means to have talent. These four-legged actors will hold you in their paws as they demonstrate what it takes to succeed in Hollywood. Do not miss this opportunity to see your favorite furry celebrities from *The Proposal*, *Ace Ventura Pet Detective* and *Hotel for Dogs*.

1. ✯ As you look around the Soundstage for the Universal's Animal Actors, what does the sign for today's special read?
    a. Chicken fingers   c. Chicken strips
    b. Chicken tenders   d. Fried chicken
2. ✯✯ Which of the animal actors has dressing room B1 according to the sign board?
    a. Dusty   c. Olympus
    b. Sparky   d. Daisy
3. ✯✯ Find the stack of crates on the left side of the stage. Which of these is not one of the labels on the crates?
    a. Seed   c. Kibble
    b. Catnip   d. Treats

The Great Universal Studios Hollywood Scavenger Hunt

4. ☆ When Sparky arrives on set to show you how to fly to an actor, what item does she need to recognize?
   a. A coin
   b. A flag
   c. A dollar bill
   d. A treat

5. ☆ How does the trainer tell the audience volunteer to retrieve their item after Sparky takes it from them?
   a. Wait till the end of the show
   b. Flap really hard and fly down to get it
   c. Walk to the front of the stage
   d. Nothing, it is a tip

6. ☆☆ As you watch the hawk and owls on the stage, what family of birds are these a part of?
   a. Parrot
   b. Vulture
   c. Eagle
   d. Raptor

7. ☆ How do your animal trainers demonstrate how to get film of an animal in flight?
   a. Tie the camera to the bird
   b. CGI filming
   c. A giant fan
   d. Train the bird to fly standing still

8. ☆ What does the trainer call the small round disc that signals the dog where he should stand?
   a. Mark
   b. Coin
   c. Circle
   d. Check

9. ☆ What item of clothing does the dog bring out on the second attempt of the dog training segment?
   a. Tie
   b. Brassiere
   c. Hat
   d. Sock

10. ☆☆ During the obstacle course demonstration, which of these is *not* one of the obstacles the dogs must maneuver through?
    a. Jump human obstacle
    b. Through the tunnel
    c. Weave through poles
    d. Jump over tires

11. ★ When the dog is lying on the stage, what does the trainer suggest they do?
    a. Take an X-ray
    b. Get the veterinarian
    c. Run a cat scan
    d. Give him more treats
12. ★ As the chicken jumps on the Today's Specials sign, what does she change the sign to read?
    a. Closed
    b. Vegetarian sandwich
    c. Vegetable soup
    d. Cesar salad
13. ★★ Before you leave the Animal Actors Stage area, stop to read some of the notices posted on the bulletin board to the left side of the stage. If you read the UAA call sheet, which of these is *not* one of the names you see?
    a. Fi Fi
    b. Naia
    c. Jacqui
    d. Charlotte
14. ★★ As you read the list of scenes pinned to the bulletin board, what is the scene number for the guinea pig entrance?
    a. Scene eleven
    b. Scene nine
    c. Scene ten
    d. Scene twenty-three
15. ★★ If you read the fan letters posted on the board, which famous animal star gave this show two fins up?
    a. Nemo
    b. Jaws
    c. Willie
    d. Flipper
16. ★★ Look for the notice for auditions with several tear off phone numbers. What is the name of the production they are looking for actors to perform in?
    a. Jaws 28
    b. Flea Wars
    c. Tunnel to Freedom: A Dogs Escape
    d. Kitty vs Pup

Did you know?

One of the letters you see attached to the board is from the world-famous shark, Jaws. Read his letter and see how he describes his various talents. He can be found scaring tourists around Amity Island on the famous studio tour.

Did you know?

At the end of the show, you can go down to the stage and meet the animals that performed during the show.

WaterWorld®

The arena for the WaterWorld® stunt show has had several incarnations over the years. The first show in this arena was *the A-Team* stunt show which premiered in 1984 and finished its run in 1987. This was followed by *The Miami Vice* stunt show in 1987, finishing it's run in 1995. The current show premiered in 1995 and still runs twenty-three years later.

1. ★★★ As the show begins, your narrator give the backstory of WaterWorld. What event caused the flooding of the earth according to your narrator?
    a. Massive rain storm
    b. Tsunami
    c. Ocean earthquake
    d. Polar ice caps melted

2. ★★ What is the metal structure called that the survivors of the global flooding live on?
    a. Atoll
    b. Scaffolding
    c. Framework
    d. Archway

3. ★★ When the sentry sees the flare and they open the gates, what is the name of the woman that they allow access to the structure?
    a. Catherine
    b. Brooke
    c. Helen
    d. Maria

4. ★★ What does she bring to show the survivors of the flood?
   a. Pure oil
   b. Fresh water
   c. Fresh fruit
   d. Pure dirt
5. ★★★ What is the name of the evil crime boss that breaks into the survivor's home looking for Helen?
   a. The Mariner
   b. The Deacon
   c. The Admiral
   d. The Bishop
6. ★ What are the henchmen for the Deacon called?
   a. Robbers
   b. Smokers
   c. Drinkers
   d. Beaters
7. ★ What sort of sporting equipment does the crime boss carry with him?
   a. A baseball bat
   b. A Cricket bat
   c. A golf club
   d. Tennis racket
8. ★★ Who told the deacon about dry land?
   a. The Provider
   b. The Master
   c. The Worshiped one
   d. The Enabler
9. ★★★ Which of these is *not* one of the ways the Deacon will use dryland?
   a. Drill it
   b. Tax it
   c. Drive it
   d. Build on it
10. ★★ The mariner is half human, half what species?
    a. Dolphin
    b. Octopus
    c. Fish
    d. Whale
11. ★ How do the smokers kill the atoller who does not know the way to dryland?
    a. Throw him off the Atoll
    b. Drop him in toxic waste
    c. Drown him
    d. Shoot him

12. ★★ When it appears the deacon and Helen are the only ones left on the Atoll; the deacon changes his vision for dryland as a pilgrimage for two as what?
    a. Roommates
    b. Boyfriend and girlfriend
    c. Lovers
    d. Husband and wife

13. ★★ How does Helen kill the deacon as he is fighting with the mariner?
    a. Set him on fire
    b. Stabs him
    c. Shoots him
    d. Drowns him

Did you know?

The actors that perform the stunts for WaterWorld are actual working actors in Hollywood. Listen as they are introduced at the end of the show to learn about the body of work for each actor.

Springfield

Hang out with your friends the Simpson's when you step into Springfield on the upper lot. Explore the games of Krustyland or stop in the Kwik-E-Mart for an ice-cold Squishee. Get a picture with Bart, Lisa Homer and Marge or dare to meet Sideshow Bob. Wind up your day with a refreshing drink at Moe's Tavern as you immerse yourself in the world of the Simpson's.

1. ★★★ As you enter Springfield, read the town sign to the left of the entrance. What does the yellow sign with the purple emblem represent at the bottom of this sign?
   a. Treehouse of Horror
   b. Springfield Police
   c. The Stonecutters
   d. Krustyland

2. ★ Find the Springfield emblem showing Jebediah Springfield and finish the motto, "A noble spirit _____ the smallest man."
   a. Empowers
   b. Enables
   c. Disables
   d. Embiggens

3. ★★ In what year was Springfield established?
   a. 1896
   b. 1796
   c. 1986
   d. 1679

4. ★★ Walk across the street to The Androids Dungeon. What event is the reason this shop is closed so Comic Book Guy can attend?
   a. Bi monthly Sci Fi Con
   b. Monthly D&D meeting
   c. Cosplay Convention
   d. Dinner with mother
5. ★ Look in the window of The Androids Dungeon, which of these comic book titles is to the left of the baseball cards on display?
   a. Radioactive Man
   b. Zebra Girl
   c. Fall Out Boy
   d. Zoidzilla
6. ★ Which business stands above The Androids Dungeon?
   a. Moe's Tavern
   b. Duff Brewery
   c. Krustyland
   d. Krustylu Studios

Did you know?
Next door to The Androids Dungeon is Lard Lad Donuts. Get your Big Pink and discover what Homer Simpson has been drooling over for more than twenty years.

---

7. ★★ Careful not to run into the police car crashed in front of Lard Lad Donuts. What is the license plate of the chief's car?
   a. #1CHIEF
   b. #1GOOFBALL
   c. #1DOOFUS
   d. PLCCHEF

Did you know?
Hang out with police Chief Wiggum for a quick picture and watch the lights and siren of his car alert you to danger from time to time.

The Great Universal Studios Hollywood Scavenger Hunt

8. ★★★ Look closely at the donut in the police chief's hand. How many sprinkles can you find on his donut?
   a. Six
   b. Nine
   c. Four
   d. Twelve

Krusty Burger

9. ★ As you walk into the Krusty Burger, take a look at the giant clown head above the counter. How many teeth does Krusty have?
   a. Nine
   b. Ten
   c. Eight
   d. Six

> ### Did you know?
> On the second floor, you will find a set of secret doors leading into Krusty's study. If you read some of the book titles, you will find each is the title of an episode of the Simpson's including the season and episode number.

10. ★★ Walk to the second floor of the Krusty Burger and find the right entrance to Krusty's private library. As you stop to read the titles of the volumes in the bookshelves to the left, which title is on the bottom shelf fourth book from the left?
    a. *Take my Wife, Please*
    b. *Take my Life, Please*
    c. *Miracle of Evergreen Terrace*
    d. *The Ten-Perfect Solution*

11. ★★ Continue reading the titles on the door to your left Which season does the episode Flaming Moe's come from?
    a. One
    b. Four
    c. Five
    d. Three

12. ★★ On season two, volume seven which holiday is Bart battling?
    a. Christmas
    b. Valentine's day
    c. Thanksgiving
    d. Easter
13. ★★★ In season 19, episode 10, which Simpson's character is in the title that begins "*E. Pluribus*"?
    a. Wiggum
    b. Krabappel
    c. Brockman
    d. Krusty
14. ★★ Read the volume titles on the bookshelves to the right of the doorway. Which volume sits on the third shelve down three in from the right side?
    a. *Oh Brother, Where Bart Thou*
    b. *Rosebud*
    c. *Husbands and Knives*
    d. *Funeral for a Friend*
15. ★★ On season 14 volume 3, finish the title. *Bart vs Lisa vs_____*.
    a. The second-grade
    b. The third-grade
    c. Springfield Elementary
    d. The Springfield
16. ★★★ Which of the following is the correct title on the cover of season four volume nine?
    a. *Marge gets a job*
    b. *Lisa's first word*
    c. *New kid on the block*
    d. *Mr. Plow*
17. ★★ Which name is the correct title of Season nine volume seven, *The two Mrs. _____*.
    a. Simpson's
    b. Wiggum's
    c. Nahasapeemapetilons
    d. Quimby's
18. ★★ Which of these titles is on the book on the right door in the bottom row on the left?
    a. *Kamp Krusty*
    b. *Married to the Blob*
    c. *Jazzy and the Pussycats*
    d. *Tree House of Horror Twenty-one*

The Great Universal Studios Hollywood Scavenger Hunt

19. ★ Enter Krusty's private study, and find the frame containing three Krusty Comics. Finish the line at the top of the comic books, "Hey kids! Give a hoot! _____."
    a. Don't pollute
    b. Watch the Simpsons
    c. Watch Krusty the Clown
    d. Buy this comic!
20. ★★ Nearby, find the caricature of one of the Simpsons characters as a werewolf. Which Simpsons character do you see?
    a. Homer Simpson
    b. Ned Flanders
    c. Barney Gumble
    d. Lenny Leonard
21. ★★★ As you look at the photographs on the walls, which celebrity is found holding a balloon carousel?
    a. Luke Perry
    b. Michael Jackson
    c. Sideshow Bob
    d. Ian Zering
22. ★★ What disease is featured on the poster for the 27th annual Krusty the Clown telethon?
    a. ADHD
    b. Motion Sickness
    c. Allergies
    d. Obesity
23. ★★ Stop for a moment to read the map of Krustyland framed on the wall. According to the attraction at number 11, which character is in the castle?
    a. Scratchy
    b. Mr. Teeny
    c. Itchy
    d. Krusty
24. ★★ According to the Krustyland map, what is the attraction at number 24?
    a. Krusty's haunted condo
    b. Gazebo just north of the dragon boat ride
    c. It's a long, long line!
    d. The tooth chipper

25. ★★★ As you look at the cartoon drawings along the walls, which celebrity is holding a martini glass near the corner of the room?
    a. Elizabeth Taylor
    b. Dean Martin
    c. Rodney Dangerfield
    d. Merv Griffin

Bonus question:

26. ★★★ Along this area of Krusty's library, you will find a caricature of a bald man in a lavender oval. What famous person did this character claim he was in one episode of The Simpsons?
    a. Michael Jordan
    b. Michael Jackson
    c. Samuel Jackson
    d. Randy Jackson
27. ★★ Find the framed photo of Sideshow bob holding a book, which of these is *not* one of the items on his to do list in this picture?
    a. Wash his hair
    b. Threaten Bart
    c. Buy corn
    d. Do Laundry
28. ★★★ Take a look at the cartoon drawings near the emergency exit door, which cartoon character from another series is seen near this door?
    a. Megatron
    b. Alpha 5
    c. Robbie
    d. Bender
29. ★★★ To the left of the window on the left side of the library, find the photo of Krusty with what famous singer in a red gown?
    a. Madonna
    b. Cher
    c. Bette Midler
    d. Christina Aguilera
30. ★★★ Nearby, find the caricature of Homer dangling from a rope below a helicopter type contraption. What famous person is driving this contraption?
    a. Stephen Hawking
    b. Steven Tyler
    c. Stephen Baldwin
    d. Stephen King

The Great Universal Studios Hollywood Scavenger Hunt

31. ★ What college is the framed diploma from you see hanging on the wall?
    a. Rabbi college
    b. Clown college
    c. Santa school
    d. Police academy
32. ★★★ What is the name of the puppet you see beneath the glass on the wall?
    a. Sideshow Mel
    b. Howdy Doody
    c. Ronald MacDonald
    d. Gabbo
33. ★★ Look at the cartoon drawing high above your head, which character plays the saxophone near the air vent?
    a. Bleeding Gums Murphy
    b. Bill Clinton
    c. Blind Willie Johnson
    d. Bleeding Gums O'Sullivan
34. ★★ In the corner of the room you will see a drawing of a man in a suit holding a rake, which Simpson's character is represented in the shadow behind him?
    a. Homer Simpson
    b. Krusty the Clown
    c. Sideshow Bob
    d. Barney Gumble

> **Did you know?**
>
> There are two entrances to Krusty's private study. The doorway to the left has another set of double doors. At the top of these doors is an image of Krusty the Clown.

35. ★★ On the doorway to the left of Krusty's study you will find another set of doors hidden by a bookcase. Find the book for season thirteen volume eight. Finish the title, "*Sweets and sour _____.*"
    a. Lisa
    b. Maggie
    c. Selma
    d. Marge

36. ★★ Find the book title for season three volume four. Finish the title, "*Bart the* _____."
    a. Skateboarder
    b. Murderer
    c. Tormentor
    d. Nerd

37. ★★ Continue your search of the book titles and find season eight volume two. Finish the title, "*You only _____ twice.*"
    a. Live
    b. Move
    c. Ride
    d. Haunt

38. ★★★ As you continue reading through the book titles, which of these is the title of a Simpson's episode?
    a. *N'Sync*
    b. *Backstreet Boys*
    c. *One Direction*
    d. *New Kid on the Block*

39. ★★ In season nine volume one, which city sued Homer Simpson?
    a. Los Angeles
    b. Chicago
    c. New York
    d. Philadelphia

Bonus question:

40. ★★★ Find the title for the episode *Whacking Day*, which aired in season four. Which famous singer arrives but leaves when he finds out what Whacking Day is all about?
    a. Michael Jackson
    b. James Brown
    c. Barry White
    d. Marvin Gaye

Cletus Chicken Shack

41. ★★ If you exit the Krusty Burger on the second floor, you will enter Cletus's Chicken Shack. What do the jugs scattered around the room on the second floor contain?
    a. Moonshine
    b. Grease
    c. Chicken oil
    d. Gasoline

The Great Universal Studios Hollywood Scavenger Hunt

42. ★ Find the test kitchen offerings on the wall. What sort of meat is offered with jerky?
    a. Skunk
    b. Cat
    c. Squirrel
    d. Pig
43. ★ Find the instruments for the Spuckler Family Ol' Timee Jug Band. What sort of shakers do you find behind the chicken wire?
    a. Chicken
    b. Sheep
    c. Squirrel
    d. Turkey
44. ★★★ Which Simpson's character do you find on the ceiling above your head on the second floor?
    a. Santa's Little Helper
    b. Spider Pig
    c. Snowball II
    d. Princess the Horse

> Did you know?
>
> Look at the ceiling and walls around you. You will find the hoof prints of Spider Pig trailing around the room.

45. ★★ As you walk through Cletus Chicken Shack, stop to look at some of the family pictures. Find the picture of the Spuckler children playing instruments. What barnyard animal is playing along with them?
    a. Sheep
    b. Turkey
    c. Donkey
    d. Rooster
46. ★★★ As you walk down the stairs to the first floor of Cletus' Chicken Shack, you will find a mural of Cletus and the young'uns near the ordering area. How many children do you see in the picture?
    a. Fifteen
    b. Twenty
    c. Twenty-three
    d. Twenty-five
47. ★ Read the menu board for Cletus Chicken Shack. What do they call the chicken strip meal #2?
    a. Chicken fingers
    b. Chicken thumbs
    c. Chicken feet
    d. Chicken young'un's

> **Did you know?**
> Exit Cletus Chicken Shack and listen for the chickens clucking in the crate on the porch.

48. ★ Which of these items can be found in the sacks sitting on the porch of Cletus' Chicken Shack?
    a. Day old beaks
    b. Week old talons
    c. Month old cartilage
    d. Fresh snouts
49. ★★ Make your way back to the Krusty Burger and find the drive through window on the side of the entrance. What is the correct name of the employee working the window?
    a. Homer Simpson
    b. Abraham Simpson
    c. Jeremy Freedman
    d. Nelson Muntz
50. ★★★ What is the correct name of the Simpson's character on the employee of the month sign?
    a. Hans Moleman
    b. Moe Syzlak
    c. Herbert Powell
    d. Kearney Zzyzwicz
51. ★★ Which of these is *not* one of the burgers offered at the Krusty Burger according to the menu?
    a. Mother nature burger
    b. Krusty burger
    c. Clogger burger
    d. Almost a burger

Bonus Question

52. ★★★ Next to the Krusty Burger is the window for King Toot's Music. What is the name of the Simpsons character you see in the window holding a baton?
    a. Bleeding Gums Murphy
    b. Mr. Largo
    c. Mr. Costington
    d. Gil Gunderson

Moe's Tavern

Take a seat at the bar of Moe's Tavern for a cold Duff beer or the famous Flaming Moe.

53. ★ Enter Moe's Tavern and find the love tester in the corner of the room, which of these is the highest rating on this novelty machine?
    a. Hot Tamale
    b. Hubba Hubba
    c. Grandpa
    d. Casanova

Bonus Question

54. ★★★ Which Simpson's character was trapped in the love tester machine on the episode titled *The Simpson's Spin off Showcase*?
    a. Homer Simpson
    b. Bart Simpson
    c. Grandpa Simpson
    d. Moe

> **Did you know?**
> Stop and take a picture with the life size Barney Gumble in Moe's Tavern. Notice his beer mug is almost empty.

55. ★ Read the Pennants around the room. What is the name of the baseball team from Shelbyville?
    a. Shelbyvillians
    b. Shelly's
    c. Goofballs
    d. Isotopes
56. ★ Take a look at the framed picture of Homer's softball team. What is the number on Homer's jersey?
    a. Sixty-two
    b. Twenty-six
    c. Thirteen
    d. Seven

57. ★★ Look behind the bar at Moe's Tavern at the bottles on display. Which of these is the liquor with Side Show Bob on the bottle?
    a. Pruno
    b. Beeno
    c. Almost red wine
    d. Fancy Pants Whiskey

58. ★★ What is the name of the Whiskey with Barney on the bottle?
    a. Barneys Choice
    b. Whiskey bottle
    c. Alkie's Choice
    d. Fat Tony's Choice

> ### Did you know?
> Sit on the left side of the bar and answer lift the receiver of the large red telephone with the yellow buttons. Listen as Bart Simpson crank calls Moe's Tavern

---

59. ★★★ When you exit Moe's Tavern, look up at Springfield Penitentiary above you. Side Show Bob is escaping once again. What is his prison number on his jumpsuit?
    a. 91608
    b. 90028
    c. 26401
    d. 24601

60. ★★ How many prison cell windows do you see on Springfield Penitentiary?
    a. Thirty-five
    b. Sixty
    c. Thirty
    d. Thirty-two

61. ★★ Across the road, standing in front of the Duff Brewery you will find the seven Duffs. Which of these is *not* one of the seven Duffs?
    a. Queasy
    b. Edgy
    c. Drunky
    d. Remorseful

The Great Universal Studios Hollywood Scavenger Hunt

Bonus question:

62. ★★★ Find the Springfield Nuclear Power Plant. What is the name of the mascot you see on the sign in front of this business?
    a. Ernie Energy
    b. Smiling Joe Fission
    c. Freddy Fission
    d. Peter Plutonium
63. ★ How many days has the Springfield Nuclear Power Plant gone without an accident?
    a. Two
    b. Four
    c. Five-hundred thirty
    d. Nine hundred

> **Did you know?**
> Find the red button near the door of the power plant. The barrels leaking nuclear waste will start to shake and, if you hit the button just right, you could create a full meltdown of the plant.

64. ★ Peek in the window of the Springfield Nuclear Power Plant and find the safety coordinator is gone. Where has he gone according to the note on his chair?
    a. Getting donuts
    b. Personal day
    c. Taking a nap
    d. Gone fission
65. ★ Above Cletus Chicken Shack you will find the Aztec theater. What movie is being played?
    a. *Revenge of the Space Mutants*
    b. *The Itchy and Scratchy Movie*
    c. *Mr. Smith goes to Washington*
    d. *Ernest goes somewhere Cheap*
66. ★ Find the office for Dr. Nick. What has he been for over two decades as you read his office door?
    a. Unlicensed
    b. Practicing
    c. In medical school
    d. Unconvicted

67. ★★★ What are the names of the two cops you see standing in front of the Springfield Police Station?
    a. Lenny and Squiggy
    b. Ralph and Clancy
    c. Eddie and Lou
    d. Nelson and Eddie
68. ★★ Which character from the Simpson's is seen trying to escape from the window of the Springfield Police Department?
    a. Hank Scorpio
    b. Snake
    c. Fat Tony
    d. Cecil Terwilliger
69. ★ On the awning for Disco Stu's you will find a record album, what is the song title on the record?
    a. *Billy, don't be a Hero*
    b. *Hooked on a Feeling*
    c. *The day the music died*
    d. *One Hit Wonder*

Bonus question:

70. ★★ Across the road you will find the Springfield Department of Motor Vehicles. What is the name of the iguana you see on Selma's shoulder?
    a. Snowball
    b. Santa's little helper
    c. Jub-Jub
    d. Patty
71. ★★★ As you look at the long line of people waiting at the Springfield DMV, which character is standing first in this line?
    a. Sideshow Mel
    b. Mr. Teeny
    c. Sideshow Bob
    d. Hershel Krustofski
72. ★ Notice the now serving sign at number four. What number does Hans Moleman hold in his hand?
    a. four
    b. Ten thousand four hundred ninety-seven
    c. Six hundred forty-seven
    d. Twelve

73. ★★ As you read the eye chart on the wall, what does the sixth line down read?
    a. GSMALLER
    b. BLIND
    c. THEN YOU ARE GOING
    d. To us you are mere ants, ants!

Bonus Question:

74. ★★★ As you look at the long line of Springfield residents waiting at the DMV, what is the name of the Springfielder holding two babies?
    a. Shari Bobbins
    b. Lindsey Naegle
    c. Paris Texan
    d. Brandine Spuckler
75. ★★ Find the wanted poster on the wall of the DMV, what is the name of this wanted man?
    a. Crazy old man
    b. Apu Nahasapeemapetilonn
    c. Homer Simpson
    d. Disco Stu
76. ★★ Which two Simpson's characters work at the Springfield Department of Motor Vehicles?
    a. Kirk and LuAnn Houten
    b. Sarah and Clancy Wiggum
    c. Kang and Kodos
    d. Patty and Selma Bouvier
77. ★★★ Periodically, you will find Sideshow Bob outside the Springfield DMV meeting park guests. What is the prison number on Sideshow Bob's jumpsuit?
    a. 58008
    b. 90210
    c. 24601
    d. 12345

> **Did you know?**
>
> Stop to take a picture with Milhouse as he sits on the bench outside the Kwik-E-Mart sipping on an ice-cold Squishee.

The Kwik-E-Mart

78. ★ Which Simpson's character do you see trapped in the window of the Kwik-E-Mart?
    a. Maggie
    b. Bart
    c. Lisa
    d. Milhouse

Bonus question

79. ★★★ What celebrity took over for Apu in season five of the Simpsons to research a movie role of a convenience store clerk?
    a. Steve Carrell
    b. Alec Baldwin
    c. Luke Perry
    d. James Woods

80. ★★ As you continue to look in the window of the Kwik-E-Mart, read the box for Krusty O's. What does every box contain?
    a. A full pound of sugar
    b. Flesh eating bacteria
    c. Wood chips for fiber
    d. Marshmallow cigarettes

81. ★ Find the Tofu shampoo in the window. Which of these is *not* one of the scents offered?
    a. Berry
    b. Tandoori chicken
    c. Chow Mein
    d. Brussels sprout

The Great Universal Studios Hollywood Scavenger Hunt

82. ★ On the package of Dry Diapers, how much is the capacity of each diaper?
    a. Five ounces
    b. iHiltoHiltohhFive cups
    c. Five pounds
    d. Five liters

Bonus Question

83. ★★★ What is the name of the baby that is featured on the package for Dry Diapers?
    a. Baby Gerald
    b. Baby Maggie
    c. Baby Anoop
    d. Baby Kearney
84. ★ What flavor Squishee is being advertised on the window of the Kwik-E-Mart?
    a. Mango Chutney Explosion
    b. Anchovy peach
    c. Bacon lime
    d. Raspberry Jalapeno
85. ★★ According to the package for Krusty Logs, what extra does this product include now?
    a. Extra bugs
    b. Extra leaves
    c. Extra bark
    d. Extra moss
86. ★★ Find the package of Krusty's Dinner on a Stick. According to the packaging, how long is the nuclear shelf life of this product?
    a. One week
    b. Ten thousand years
    c. One million years
    d. Two days
87. ★★ If you read the label for Krusty Kough Syrup, what is this product the secret ingredient for?
    a. The Flaming Homer
    b. The Squishee
    c. The Flaming Moe
    d. The Krusty Burger

Bonus Question:

88. ★★★ Among the many products advertised in the Kwik-E-Mart window, find the package with the cat on the front. If you watch The Simpsons, what is the name of this character?
    a. Santa's Little Helper
    b. Laddie
    c. Snowball II
    d. Princess

> **Did you know?**
> Enter and look around the Kwik E Mart and you will find small personalized license plates. They also sell the famous Bort license plate found in the Simpson's episode Itchy and Scratchy Land.

89. ★★ When you enter The Kwik-E-Mart, read the sign outlining the Kwik E Mart policy on checks near the cash register. Which of these is *not* one of the options you see?
    a. No third-party checks
    b. No counterfeit checks
    c. Stripes work with checks
    d. No out of state checks

90. ★ As you explore the Kwik-E-Mart, read some of the advertisements along the walls. Finish the heat lamp dog sign, "Featuring dangerously _____ hot dogs."
    a. Old
    b. Spicy
    c. Large
    d. Small

91. ★ Find the Jack Pot sign within the Kwik-E-Mart. What does this sign say you are wasting if you do not play?
    a. Your money
    b. Your life
    c. Your day
    d. Your luck

The Great Universal Studios Hollywood Scavenger Hunt

92. ★ Find the Squishee machine within the Kwik-E-Mart. Which Simpsons character is sitting atop this machine?
    a. Bart
    b. Lisa
    c. Milhouse
    d. Nelson
93. ★ Exit the back door of the Kwik-E-Mart and turn to the left. There is a stack of beer bottles on the ground against the wall. How many beer bottles do you see?
    a. Eight
    b. Ten
    c. Six
    d. Seven
94. ★ According to the No Dumping sign behind the Kwik-E-Mart, what is the Springfield code for this sign?
    a. 77621
    b. 58008
    c. 24601
    d. 92782
95. ★★ If you step out the back door of the Kwik-E-Mart, you will find a trash can with the words Stupid Head spray painted on it. Whose picture do you see painted on this can?
    a. Monty Burns
    b. Homer Simpson
    c. Barney Gumble
    d. Ralph Wiggum

The Simpson's Ride

> **Did you know?**
>
> Before you walk through the open mouth of Krusty the Clown, stop and look directly above you. Krusty has a uvula dangling down from the roof of his mouth.

96. ★★ As you approach The Simpson's Ride, find the height measurement indicator. What Simpson's duo appear on the indicator?
    a. Eddie and Lou
    b. Abe and Mona
    c. Side Show Bob and Side Show Mel
    d. Itchy and Scratchy

> **Did you know?**
>
> In front of The Simpson's Ride you will see the Simpson's family high above you in a ride car. There is a red button mounted just below them. If you push the button absolutely nothing happens, it is just there for fun.

97. ★★ After you enter the queue, Find the park map for Krustyland. Finish the title for number fifteen on the map, "Captain Dinosaurs Pirate _____."
    a. All singing and dancing revue
    b. Merchandise advertisement
    c. Rip-off
    d. Robotic ride

98. ★★ In Krusty's Haunted Condo, there are 999 of what sort of creatures?
    a. Fake ghosts
    b. Robotic zombies
    c. Sheets dressed up like ghosts
    d. Unhappy teen employees

99. ★★ On the map find and finish the attraction name "Moe's Tunnel of _____."
    a. The next best thing to love
    b. Shame and rejection
    c. Groping in the dark
    d. Spooky stuff in the dark

100. ★★ The last item on the list is number forty, "Get _____ by Kang and Kodos."
     a. Probed
     b. Abducted
     c. Slimed
     d. Taken away

The Great Universal Studios Hollywood Scavenger Hunt

101. ★★ Read some of the posters for the attractions you will find at Krustyland throughout the queue area. Which Simpson's character is featured as the mummy on the poster for Screamatorium of Dr. Frightmarestein?
    a. Barney
    b. Cletus
    c. Milhouse
    d. Side Show Bob

102. ★★ Which of Bart and Lisa's friends are featured on the poster for Radioactive Man the Ride?
    a. Bart and Milhouse
    b. Nelson and Kearney
    c. Sherri and Terri
    d. Martin and Ralph

103. ★★★ What Simpsons character is featured on the Krusty's Wet and Smoky Stunt Show poster?
    a. Troy McClure
    b. Radioactive man
    c. Sideshow Mel
    d. McBain

104. ★★★ Which is these ladies of Springfield is *not* found on the poster for the Isotop-ettes?
    a. Lurleen Lumpkin
    b. Patty Bouvier
    c. Paris Texan
    d. Edna Krabappel

105. ★ What sort of simulator can you find in Krustyland as you read the posters?
    a. Amusement park
    b. Yard work
    c. Presidential election
    d. Larry Totter Wizard

106. ★★ As you enter the pre-ride area, look around at the different booths. Which Simpson's character mans the information booth?
    a. Abe Simpson
    b. Jasper
    c. Old Jewish Man
    d. Hans Moleman

107. ★★ Read some of the brochures that sit atop the counter of the information booth. What do you get for free with a drink at Moe's Tavern?
    a. Panda
    b. Date with Barney
    c. Expired pickled egg
    d. Date with Moe

108. ★★ Find and finish the title of the brochure for "A Hot Time in the Old _____."
    a. Broken down drive-in
    b. Small town
    c. Tire yard
    d. Church basement
109. ★ Which attraction is slated for demolition according to the information sign?
    a. The Yard Work Simulator
    b. The Traumanator Coaster
    c. Radioactive man the Ride
    d. Poochies Toddler Kennel
110. ★ Find the framed picture of the Krustyland worker in the pre-show area. What is the name of the krew member for this ride?
    a. Side Show Robert
    b. Side Show Krusty
    c. Side Show Barney
    d. Side Show Homer
111. ★ As you read the list of items at the snack bar, which of these is *not* one of the candies available?
    a. Cotton candy
    b. Linen candy
    c. Stringy candy
    d. Flannel candy
112. ★ What is the fried item on the menu at the snack bar?
    a. Fried sushi
    b. Fried chewing gum
    c. Fried Plantain
    d. Fried sugar
113. ★ What attraction is boarded up and closed for repairs within the pre-show area?
    a. Happy Little Elves in Panda Land
    b. Madam Manjula the Future Looker-atter
    c. Screamatorium of Dr. Frightmarestein
    d. Yard Work Simulator
114. ★ Near the snack bar you will find the Hi Striker game. What is the top level you reach when you ring the bell?
    a. Krusty
    b. Superhero
    c. Schlub
    d. Regular hero

The Great Universal Studios Hollywood Scavenger Hunt

115. ★★ On the Itchy and Scratchy wheel of pain, which word is paired with eyeballs?
     a. Twist
     b. Gouge
     c. Pop
     d. Switch

> **Did you know?**
> The Simpson's Ride uses the same building as the predecessor, The Back to the Future Ride. The engineers used the exact same ride movements, animating the action on the screen to match the previous ride movements.

116. ★★ What body part is paired with pinched on the Itchy and Scratchy Wheel of Pain?
     a. Earlobe
     b. Bellybutton
     c. Uvula
     d. Eyeball

117. ★★ Look for the tarot cards surrounding Madam Manjula's the Future Looker-atter. Which Simpson's character is seen on the card for death?
     a. Death
     b. Mr. Burns
     c. Devil Flanders
     d. Bart Simpson

118. ★★★ As you watch some of the advertisements for Krustyland on the overhead monitors, what should you watch out for on the Krusty's Stagecoach Stampede attraction?
     a. Groping undertaker
     b. Inverted loop
     c. Malfunctioning robot cowboys
     d. Horse apples

119. ★★★ As the monitor shows you more attractions at Krustyland, what is the reason for the Haunted Condo being closed?
     a. Dusting cobwebs
     b. Annual exorcisms
     c. Bi-weekly extermination
     d. Annual ghostbusting

120. ★★ What is the wait time for Captain Dinosaur's Pirate Rip-off according to the monitor overhead?
    a. Four hours
    b. Two hours
    c. Five hours
    d. Seven hours
121. ★★★ Read the sign looking for a dancer to perform in the Four Food Groups Singing Spectacular. What piece of fruit are they looking for?
    a. Tomato
    b. Grapefruit
    c. Kumquat
    d. Lemon
122. ★★ As you read the advertisement for the Krustyland Fudge Factory, they will caramel anything. What shaped object is the adult man holding covered in caramel?
    a. Hammer
    b. Football
    c. Hamburger
    d. Pineapple
123. ★★ What sort of cruise will you take on Captain Queasy's attraction coming soon to Krustyland?
    a. Drunk
    b. Barf
    c. Hurricane
    d. Rubber dinghy
124. ★★ What is the latest snack sensation at Krustyland according to the advertisements?
    a. Clown nose
    b. Clown feet
    c. Clown kabobs
    d. Clown hair
125. ★★ As you pre-show video begins, you see Krusty the Clown talking to you. How much longer does he say you will be in line?
    a. Forty-five hours
    b. Forty-five days
    c. Forty-five minutes
    d. Four hours
126. ★★ As you take your seat and your ride begins, which Simpson's character says, "You're all gonna die."?
    a. Nelson
    b. Side Show Bob
    c. Krusty
    d. Homer

The Great Universal Studios Hollywood Scavenger Hunt

127. ★★ As you ride through the dinosaurs that begin to crash, what does Homer say he hates?
     a. Theme parks
     b. Dinosaurs
     c. Chain reactions
     d. Animated whos-it-whats
128. ★ What animal does Bart ride trying to save you from the water show?
     a. Dolphin
     b. Giant squid
     c. Sea lion
     d. Killer whale
129. ★ Which Simpson's character saves you from Sideshow Bob?
     a. Snake
     b. Side Show Mel
     c. Mr. Teeny
     d. Maggie
130. ★★ What does Sideshow Bob offer Maggie Simpson if she destroys Springfield?
     a. A giant bottle
     b. Her pacifier
     c. A nap
     d. Too be his minion
131. ★★ What reason does Marge give for Maggie getting the tourists out of her mouth?
     a. They're dirty
     b. No snacking between meals
     c. You don't know where they've been
     d. You might choke
132. ★★ Which Simpsons characters surprise the Simpson's after the think they are home?
     a. Kang and Kodos
     b. Fang and Kiddos
     c. Side Show Bob and Maggie
     d. Kirk and LuAnne

---

133. ★ After you exit the Simpson's Ride, walk around the midway games. At the Dunk and Flunk, which character is seen with a dunce cap on his head?
     a. Ralph Wiggum
     b. Bart Simpson
     c. Nelson Muntz
     d. Martin Prince

134. ★ At the Help Santa's Little Helper game, what number does Santa's Little Helper wear on his jacket?
    a. Eighty
    b. Eighty-eight
    c. Eight
    d. Eleven
135. ★★ At the Strike 3 game, what is the name of the character seen on the sign?
    a. Cocoa Bean
    b. Lard Lad
    c. Capital City Goofball
    d. Smiling Joe Fission

Lower Lot

Take a ride through time where dinosaurs roam free, save the planet from alien take over or ride through the ancient ruins of The Mummy's tomb on the lower lot.

Revenge of the Mummy

Enter an ancient temple to discover that Imhotep lives in this world. Run for your life to save your soul from an eternity in the Revenge of the Mummy.

Did you know?

As you walk through the queue for Revenge of the Mummy and come to the entrance to the building stop at the door with a hole just big enough for your hand to fit through, do you dare surrender your hand and see what you may find?

> ### Did you know?
> As you enter the temple for Revenge of the Mummy from the Express queue, you will come across the famed book of the dead. If you have the courage to reach out to touch it you may find yourself in for a big surprise.

1. ★★ As you enter your ride vehicle and begin your journey, you will find one of the locals attempting to warn you about Imhotep. What are his final words before he is consumed by scarab beetles?
   - a. Turn back!
   - b. Imhotep lives!
   - c. You are doomed!
   - d. It is too dangerous!

> ### Did you know?
> As you watch the dead come to life be sure to look above your head as one of the mummies will come through the ceiling.

2. ★ As Imhotep appears, what form does his face take?
   - a. Sand
   - b. Human
   - c. Water
   - d. Scarab beetles

3. ★★ What does Imhotep promise you will savor if you serve him?
   - a. The treasure of the temple
   - b. The lives of the dead
   - c. The riches of eternal life
   - d. Life till the end of time

4. ★★ The last thing you see on your journey will be Imhotep standing above you chanting. Finish this statement you hear, "Now your _____ belong to me!"
   - a. Lives
   - b. Bodies
   - c. Freedom
   - d. Souls

The Great Universal Studios Hollywood Scavenger Hunt

> ### Did you know?
> The Revenge of the Mummy rollercoaster was brought to Universal Studios Hollywood after the great success of the 1999 film *The Mummy* starring Brendan Fraser. This was the first film for writer director Stephen Sommers, which became a blockbuster for Universal.

Jurassic World

> ### Did you know?
> The Jurassic World attraction is based on the 2015 film *Jurassic World* starring Chris Pratt. This attraction has been updated from the original Jurassic Park attractions that opened in 1996.

5. ★★ As you work your way through the queue for the Jurassic World attraction, stop to read some of the signs. If you read the sign for the Mosasaurus, what lizard is this dinosaur related to?
   a. Mexican Bearded Lizard
   b. Gila Monster
   c. Komodo Dragon
   d. Nile Monitor

6. ★★ Find the sign for Blue the Velociraptor. What is the bite force of this powerful animal?
   a. 10,000 Newtons
   b. 8,000 Newtons
   c. 3,000 Newtons
   d. 80,000 Newtons

7. ★★ In which era of time did the Velociraptor exist?
   a. Triassic
   b. Early Jurassic
   c. Later Cretaceous
   d. Early Cretaceous

8. ★★ As you read the sign for the Tyrannosaurus Rex, how many pounds of food do they eat per day?
   a. 308 pounds
   b. 803 pounds
   c. 380 pounds
   d. 830 pounds
9. ★★ According to the Tyrannosaurus Rex sign, how tall on average were these dinosaurs?
   a. 44.29 feet
   b. 17.06 feet
   c. 6.16 feet
   d. 5.2 feet
10. ★★ As you read the sign for the Stegosaurus, what does this name mean?
    a. Shingled lizard
    b. Spiny lizard
    c. Roofed lizard
    d. Dangerous lizard
11. ★★ Watch the video screens for Jurassic park, how many years in the making does your guide claim this attraction took to create?
    a. Sixty-five million
    b. Six million
    c. Sixty-five thousand
    d. Sixty-five years
12. ★★★ As you watch Claire being interviewed, which dinosaur enclosure is she and the interviewer standing in front of?
    a. Stegosaurus
    b. Indominus
    c. Tyrannosaurus Rex
    d. Velociraptor

Bonus question:

13. ★★★ As you watch Claire's interview, Owen walks into the shot. What is the name of the actor that plays Owen?
    a. Jeff Goldblum
    b. Chris Pratt
    c. Tom Selleck
    d. Owen Wilson
14. ★★ As you watch the segment on the Mosasaurus, how long are these aquatic dinosaurs?
    a. Fifty feet
    b. Seventy feet
    c. Twenty feet
    d. Sixty feet

The Great Universal Studios Hollywood Scavenger Hunt

> **Did you know?**
> This water ride will get everyone in the boat extremely wet. There is no area of the boat that is dryer than any other area. This is a very refreshing ride on a hot Southern California day.

15. ✯✯ As your ride begins, your narrator advises you to watch out for the new baby of which dinosaur breed?
    a. Brachiosaurus
    b. Tyrannosaurus
    c. Stegosaurus
    d. Velociraptor

> **Did you know?**
> As you travel through the predator cove, you will notice a very violent scene playing out around the Indominus enclosure. This is a very intense scene and may startle younger guests.

16. ✯✯✯ As you travel into the Tyrannosaurus Rex area, which dinosaur sprays your boat?
    a. Dilophosaurus
    b. Europasaurus
    c. Aquilops
    d. Tethyshadros

17. ✯ What is the name of the velociraptor you see to the right side of the boat as you travel through the Tyrannosaurus area?
    a. Echo
    b. Blue
    c. Charlie
    d. Delta

> **Did you know?**
> The Full figure Indominus Rex is the most advanced animated robotic figure currently in use.

Transformers: The Ride 3D

Join Optimus Prime and the freedom fighters as you protect the AllSpark from the Decepticons. Travel through the city as you race against time to save the world from being destroyed while keeping your team from falling into the hands of Megatron.

18. ★★★ As you enter the NEST you will find an ancient hieroglyphics tablet with the Transformers language imprinted on it. What is this language called?
    a. Cybertronian
    b. Sindarin
    c. Klingon
    d. Na'Vi
19. ★ As you enter the NEST find the authorized personal warning sign. Unauthorized presence constitutes a breach of what?
    a. Protocol
    b. Facilities
    c. Government procedure
    d. Security
20. ★★ As you enter the facility you will be greeted by Sonya Bradley on the monitors, what is her official title?
    a. Security enforcement
    b. Alien/Human relations
    c. Hero recruitment officer
    d. Human engineering
21. ★★ As you hear the general speaking from the monitors, what does the S in NEST stand for?
    a. Superior
    b. Subordinate
    c. Space
    d. Species

The Great Universal Studios Hollywood Scavenger Hunt

> **Did you know?**
> The NEST facility has many buttons and switches surrounding you. Feel free to play with these as you walk by, they are designed to keep you busy during your time in the queue.

22. ★★★ As you look around at the controls in the first room you come to, find the chart of Transformers silhouettes. What is the name of the transformer in the top row, second from the left?
    a. Optimus Prime
    b. Bumblebee
    c. Sidewinder
    d. Rampage
23. ★★★ Continue your scan of the Transformer silhouettes. What is the name of the image on the bottom row, third from the left?
    a. Rampage
    b. Ravage
    c. Ratchet
    d. Frenzy
24. ★ As you listen to the history of the Transformers, how was their home planet of Cybertron destroyed?
    a. Meteor hit
    b. Collision with another planet
    c. War
    d. Metal mining
25. ★ What do the Decepticons seek on Earth?
    a. Uranium
    b. The AllSpark
    c. Sam Witwicky
    d. Mikaela Banes
26. ★★ What item does the transformer call you out for having in your possession as you watch on the monitor?
    a. Ice cream
    b. Cotton candy
    c. A pretzel
    d. A churro
27. ★ As Megatron intercepts the signal, what name does he call you with his last warning?
    a. Weeds
    b. Infidels
    c. Insects
    d. Slaves

28. ★★ As you enter your ride vehicle and begin your adventure, you will come across many Decepticons that will try to annihilate you and your fellow passengers. Which Decepticon traps you in his vortex while you try to evade Megatron?
    a. Devastator
    b. Overkill
    c. Ravage
    d. Scavenger
29. ★ When Evac ask, "What do we do?", what is Megatron's response?
    a. Run while you can
    b. Give the AllSpark to me
    c. Beg for mercy
    d. Time to die
30. ★ Which transformer saves you when you are falling off the building?
    a. Optimus Prime
    b. Bumblebee
    c. Ratchet
    d. Bonecrusher
31. ★ What name does Optimus call you by when he congratulates you on your mission?
    a. Autobots
    b. Decepticon destroyers
    c. Human alliance
    d. Freedom fighter

The World-famous Studio Tour

Travel through a working movie studio as you experience the backlot of Universal Studios Hollywood. From New York to Skull Island, you will have the time of your life traveling the earth while never leaving Los Angeles. If you are lucky, you may see some of your favorite stars filming your favorite movies and television shows.

The tour you are about to embark on is the foundation of the Universal Studios theme park. Founder Carl Laemmle opened the gates to the public to watch the silent films being shot for a mere twenty-five cents. For many years, guests could cheer the heroes and boo the bad guys until the advent of the talking films.

Sound changed everything for the studios, forcing them to bring filming indoors and control the sound on the outdoor sets. Rather that close the doors permanently, Universal Studios permitted bus tours to come through, allowing guests to get a view of the lot without interrupting filming.

Catherine F. Olen

It was not until 1964 that Universal Studios would open the first tram tour solely owned by Universal. The tram would take guests through the backlot with a brief stop in what is now the lower lot where many of your favorite rides are housed.

Note:

Since Universal Studios is a working movie studio, the tram tour changes daily. You may not experience everything you see in *The Great Universal Studios Hollywood Scavenger Hunt* in one visit, but keep in mind you may have a different experience in subsequent visits.

1. ★ What famous Saturday Night Live alumni is the cohost on your tram tour?
   a. Tina Fey
   b. Amy Poehler
   c. Eddie Murphy
   d. Jimmy Fallon

Did you know?

As you leave the tram load area, you will pass beneath the Simpsons Ride to your left at the top of this large hill. In the 1960's and 1970's, this area was known as the avalanche and the tram would pause as large rocks would tumble down the hill towards the tram.

While this attraction was meant to give guests a thrill, it was more entertaining as the foam rubber rocks would bounce down the hillside.

As you begin travelling down the Universal timeline, read some of the movie posters from the films that made Universal Studios famous.

The Great Universal Studios Hollywood Scavenger Hunt

> **Did you know?**
> The road you are travelling once was the site of the burning house, an attraction designed to demonstrate a control fire effect. The house was the front of a southern mansion with gas jets fueling a fire in the windows. This attraction was retired when the Backdraft attraction was created on the lower lot.

2. ★★★ As you begin travelling down the Universal Studios timeline, what is the very first movie ever filmed at Universal Studios in 1914?
    a. *All Quiet on the Western Front*
    b. *The Hunchback of Notre Dame*
    c. *Damon and Pythias*
    d. *The Aviator*

3. ★★ In what year was the Universal Studios classic, *The Hunchback of Notre Dame* filmed?
    a. 1923
    b. 1932
    c. 1964
    d. 1971

4. ★★★ On the movie poster for the Universal classic, *The Phantom of the Opera*, you will see the producers name above the movie title, what name do you see?
    a. David O. Selznick
    b. Carl Laemmle
    c. Peter Jackson
    d. Steven Spielberg

5. ★★ What famous actor starred in the 1931 classic monster film *Dracula*?
    a. Boris Karloff
    b. Long Chaney
    c. Bela Lugosi
    d. Clark Gable

6. ★★ On the movie poster for *My Little Chickadee*, what controversial film actress starred opposite W.C. Fields?
    a. Mae West
    b. Vivienne Leigh
    c. Jayne Mansfield
    d. Marilyn Monroe

7. ★ What is the name of the famous cartoon bird you see on the 1940 poster?
   a. Tweety Bird
   b. Woody Woodpecker
   c. Daffy Duck
   d. Chilly Willy
8. ★★★ Which of these actors is *not* listed on the 1941 poster for *The Wolfman*?
   a. Claude Raines
   b. Boris Karloff
   c. Lon Chaney
   d. Ralph Bellamy
9. ★★ On the 1948 movie poster for *Abbott and Costello Meet Frankenstein*, what word is spelled out in smoke at the top of the poster?
   a. Jeepers
   b. Yikes
   c. Hey Abbott
   d. Help
10. ★★ On the 1960 movie poster for *Spartacus*, how many roman coins do you see on this poster?
    a. Six
    b. Five
    c. Seven
    d. Seventeen
11. ★★ What famous director created the 1960 horror classic *Psycho* starring Anthony Perkins?
    a. Steven Spielberg
    b. John Huston
    c. Stephen Sommers
    d. Alfred Hitchcock

Did you know?

As you read the movie posters for Universal Studios films, take note that *All Quiet on the Western Front* was the first film to win the Academy Award™ for Universal.

12. ★★★ On the poster for the 1975 classic *Jaws*, which of these actor's names does *not* appear on the poster?
    a. Robert Shaw
    b. Richard Dreyfuss
    c. John Belushi
    d. Roy Scheider

The Great Universal Studios Hollywood Scavenger Hunt

13. ★★★ Which of these actors does *not* appear on the movie poster for the 1977 film *Smokey and the Bandit*?
    a. Loni Anderson
    b. Burt Reynolds
    c. Jackie Gleason
    d. Sally Field
14. ★★★ What future Academy Award™ winning actor do you see on the movie poster for the 1982 film, *Fast Times at Ridgemont High*?
    a. Tom Hanks
    b. Sean Penn
    c. Brad Pitt
    d. Adrian Brody
15. ★★ In what year was the film *Back to the Future*, starring Michael J. Fox released?
    a. 1975
    b. 1985
    c. 1995
    d. 2005

Did you know?

As you travel down the Universal Studios timeline, you will pass by a fire station. Notice this station is Fire Station 51, named for the long running 1970's television series, *Emergency!* starring Randolph Mantooth and Kevin Tighe.

Universal Studios is actually contained within Universal City which has its own fire department, police and its own mayor.

16. ★★ In what year was the first film in *The Fast and the Furious* franchise released?
    a. 1991
    b. 2005
    c. 2010
    d. 2001
17. ★★★ On the movie poster for the 1993 blockbuster film *Jurassic Park*, finish the tag line that reads, "_____ years in the making."
    a. 55 million
    b. 75 million
    c. 65 million
    d. 5 million

18. ★★★ What Academy Award™ nominated actor appears on the movie poster for the 2000 film, *Gladiator*?
    a. Russell Crowe
    b. Brad Pitt
    c. Antonio Banderas
    d. Brendan Fraser
19. ★★★ In the 2003 movie poster for *Bruce Almighty*, starring Jim Carrey, what is he holding in his hand?
    a. A yoyo
    b. A playing card
    c. A globe
    d. A crown
20. ★★ In the movie poster for the 2004 film *Ray* starring Jamie Fox, what famous Ray is this biopic about?
    a. Ray Bolger
    b. Ray Lewis
    c. Ray Charles
    d. Ray Liotta
21. ★★ On the 2014 movie poster, complete the name of this film, "*The Theory of _____.*"
    a. Nothing
    b. Everything
    c. The universe
    d. Relativity
22. ★★ On the movie poster for the 2017 animated film, *Despicable Me 3*, what is the tag line at the top of the poster?
    a. Oh brother
    b. Oh bother
    c. Super dad
    d. Gru times two

Did you know?

If you look off to your left, you will see soundstage 12, where the reality television show *The Voice* was originally filmed. Soundstage 12 is one of the biggest soundstages and the first one built at Universal for the purpose of sound filming. This soundstage housed the lab from the horror classic *Frankenstein and The Bride of Frankenstein*, as well as the mansion from *Scarface* featuring Al Pacino.

Later, Soundstage 12 was used to house the penguins lair from *Batman Returns*, the visitors center from *Jurassic Park* and Whoville from *How the Grinch Stole Christmas*.

The Great Universal Studios Hollywood Scavenger Hunt

> ### Did you know?
> You will continue your tour through the soundstages on the front lot. Look for Soundstage 27. Within this soundstage is contained one of the largest water tanks in Hollywood. A part of the ark from *Evan Almighty* starring Steve Carrell was built in this soundstage. Also house here was mission control from *Apollo 13* starring Tom Hanks and Mount Crumpit from *How the Grinch Stole Christmas*.

23. ✯✯ Your tour will take you through the soundstages and production bungalows. What were these bungalows used for prior to their current use?
    a. Prop department   c. Post production
    b. Wardrobe   d. Dressing rooms

> ### Did you know?
> The bungalows you see to the left of the tram were once a walk-through attraction for Universal Studios. The guests were allowed to walk through the dressing rooms of Doris Day, star of stage and screen. The guests also entered a small museum for costume designer Edith Head.
>
> Head designed the costumes for some of the most famous films in Hollywood. Audrey Hepburn in *Breakfast at Tiffany's*, Grace Kelly in *To Catch a Thief*, Tippi Hedren in *The Birds* and Elizabeth Taylor in *A Place in the Sun* are just a sample of the work Head created for the studios.

24. ✯ As you pass the production bungalows, you will see the silhouette of famed director Alfred Hitchcock. What number appears on Mr. Hitchcock's office?
    a. 9551   c. 5195
    b. 5519   d. 5915

> **Did you know?**
>
> As your tour continues, you will pass a small street with several homes with a short flight of stairs. This a Brownstone Street, the location for films like *The Sting*, *Home Alone 2: Lost in New York*, *Cast Away*, *The Prestige* and *Bruce Almighty*. These are just a few of the films set on this quaint part of the backlot.

25. ★★ You tour continues to one of the most famous areas of the backlot, courthouse square. What famous trilogy began right in this area of Universal Studios?
    a. *Back to the Future*
    b. *Raiders of the Lost Ark*
    c. *Star Wars*
    d. *The Godfather*

> **Did you know?**
>
> Courthouse Square has been seen in some of the most famous films ever made including, *To Kill a Mocking Bird*, *The Music Man*, *Gremlins*, *Batman and Robin* and, more recently, *Hairspray Live*.

The Great Universal Studios Hollywood Scavenger Hunt

> ### Did you know?
>
> The area known as New York Street has been the face of many iconic films throughout the history of Universal Studios. *Fate of the Furious, Bram Stokers Dracula, Captain America and The Avengers* are just a small sampling of the blockbuster films that have spent time on New York Street.
>
> This area of the backlot has been through three fires over the years in 1957, 1990 and 2008. Each time, Universal rebuilt this area to continue filming feature films. It was after the 2008 fire that director Steven Spielberg assisted in the rebuild process as a consultant to help the studio bring this area of the backlot up to date.
>
> The first incarnation of the King Kong attraction was destroyed in 2008 but gave Universal Studios the opportunity to work with director Peter Jackson on the new attraction coming up later on your tour.

26. ★★ What is the name of the island you travel to when you encounter King Kong?
    a. Amity Island
    b. Isle Nublar
    c. Skull Island
    d. Kong Island

27. ★★★ As King Kong battles prehistoric dinosaurs, what species of dinosaur does he fight to save your tram from certain death?
    a. Apatosaurus
    b. Stegosaurus
    c. Brachiosaurus
    d. Tyrannosaurus Rex

> ### Did you know?
>
> The projection screen for the *King Kong* attraction is the largest 3D projection in the world today. Prior to this attraction, the King Kong attraction was housed on New York Street with trams driving inside the sets to come face to face with the animatronic Kong.

Catherine F. Olen

> ### Did you know?
>
> Notice the dilapidated bridge just behind the King Kong attraction. This bridge has been a part of the Universal Studios backlot since the 1970's and was a part of the tour for many years. The bridge created the illusion of collapsing while traveling across on the tram. A thrill for guests of the Universal Studios tour for decades.
>
> This bridge was also featured in television shows in the 1970's and 1980's like *The Six Million Dollar Man, The Bionic Woman* and *Quantum Leap*.

> ### Did you know?
>
> If you look up the hill from the King Kong attraction, this was once part of the studio tour. The guests would be dropped off to use the restroom and get a snack at the outdoor food area. Also housed here were props from many films including an extra-large telephone from *The Incredible Shrinking Man* and a stage coach for the kids to play on. This area is now part of the upper lot and used for attractions.

28. ★ You will travel down the road the view the Universal picture cars. What make and model of car did Magnum P.I. drive?
    a. Ferrari 512
    b. Ferrari 308
    c. Ferrari 365
    d. Ferrari 411

29. ★★ Which character from the *Back to the Future* films drove the black 1946 Ford convertible you see?
    a. George Mc Fly
    b. Marty Mc Fly
    c. Biff Tannen
    d. Emmett Brown

30. ★★ What sort of power do the cars from the *Flintstones* movies use?
    a. Foot power
    b. Steam power
    c. Dinosaur power
    d. Gasoline power

The Great Universal Studios Hollywood Scavenger Hunt

> **Did you know?**
>
> In the area just below the pictures cars is a storage area for the plants and outdoor equipment used for film making. The plants are all natural and, if they are not looking green enough, they are simply spray painted with green food dye to give them a healthy green color.

31. ★★ As you cross through the *Jurassic Park* area to see some of the original cages and the mobile lab unit, what is the name of the company that ran Jurassic Park?
    a. Engine
    b. Jurassic Industries
    c. Hammond Industries
    d. Ingen

> **Did you know?**
>
> This area you are traveling through was once The Appian Way in the 1960 film *Spartacus* starring Kirk Douglas and Lawrence Olivier. The studio hired college students who were spray painted with makeup to play the Roman soldiers. If you look very closely at the scene from this classic film, you will notice some of the soldiers forgot to take off their modern watches before marching to war.

> **Did you know?**
>
> The area you are entering for the weather demonstration is almost exactly as it was when it opened in 1968. There is a long-standing rumor that the effect soaked a tram load of dignitaries at its premier including legendary western actor John Wayne.

32. ★ What famous weatherman gives you the weather for the backlot tour?
    a. Willard Scott
    b. Al Roker
    c. Adam Joseph
    d. Dallas Raines
33. ★★ What is the weather like in New York Street according to your weatherman on the video?
    a. Sunny and dry
    b. Cool and Cloudy
    c. Snow and sleet
    d. High chance of precipitation
34. ★ As your tram stops at a small Spanish village to demonstrate how weather is done in the movies, what sort of store do you see to the left of the tram at the bottom of the hill?
    a. Carneceria
    b. Panaderia
    c. Zapateria
    d. Mercado
35. ★★★ On the signpost in the Spanish village you will see the word Alto. What does this word mean in English?
    a. High
    b. Stop
    c. Yield
    d. Low

Did you know?
Since water does not show up on film, the film makers use milk to color the water and make it easier to see on screen.

Did you know?
You will cross through an area of the backlot known as Old Mexico. This area was used as the island of Tortuga in the *Pirates of the Caribbean* films.

The Great Universal Studios Hollywood Scavenger Hunt

Did you know?

As you travel away from Old Mexico towards six points Texas, look off to your right at a very small western street. This area is known as Colorado Street and is the oldest part of the Universal Studios backlot. While part of this historic site has been removed to make way for other filming, this small area is a beloved part of Universal history.

As you look down Colorado Street, notice a train engine. This train engine was used for the runaway train attraction on the tour. The tram would stop at Colorado Street and the train would come rapidly towards the tram to stop just in the nick of time.

Did you know?

As you find yourself in six points Texas, this area was named for six separate streets that met in one central area. During the silent film era of film making, Universal Studios was able to film six westerns at the same time. The studio invited the public to watch filming and, for twenty-five cents, you could cheer your favorite western heroes and get a box lunch.

Did you know?

Along six points Texas, notice the doorways on one side of the street are smaller and shorter while the doorways on the other side are taller and wider. The hero would be place in front of the smaller doorway to make them appear bigger and brawnier while the ladies would be placed in the larger doorway to appear demurer.

> ### Did you know?
> Between six points Texas and New York Street there is a large water tank used for underwater filming. One of the most famous scenes filmed here was from the film *Dragnet*, starring Tom Hanks and Dan Aykroyd. The scene where they fight the giant snake was filmed in this very spot.

> ### Did you know?
> You will see a large building with the name Edith Head Building as your tram approaches the Little Europe area of the backlot. This building houses all of the props at Universal Studios. Productions gather the items they need for filming and the studio scans a bar code located on each item to keep track of the inventory.
>
> For those interested in a sneak peek of the property warehouse, watch the film *Big Fat Liar* starring Paul Giamatti. There is a montage of the stars playing in this warehouse.

36. ✯✯✯ Universal Studios first Academy Award™ winning film was filmed in Little Europe, what is the name of this film?
    a. *Frankenstein*
    b. *The Invisible Man*
    c. *The Princess Diaries*
    d. *All Quiet on the Western Front*

37. ✯✯ As your tram stops at a large courtyard with a fountain in the center, what is the name of this area of the backlot?
    a. Court of monsters
    b. Court of history
    c. Court of miracles
    d. Frankenstein court

The Great Universal Studios Hollywood Scavenger Hunt

> ### Did you know?
> The courtyard you visited in Little Europe was named for the film, *The Hunchback of Notre Dame* starring Lon Chaney. Almost every Universal movie monster was seen in this area of the backlot including, Dracula, The Wolfman, The Mummy and Frankenstein.

> ### Did you know?
> Just before entering a soundstage, you will see a house off to the left side of the tram. This is the filming location of the show *Home and Family*. This show films five days a week and guests of the studio tour can see the hosts with their guests doing interviews from time to time.

38. ★ Your tram will give you a sneak peek into a working soundstage. What area is this soundstage currently dressed as?
    a. New York city street
    b. San Francisco subway
    c. Tokyo garden
    d. Downtown Los Angeles

39. ★★ As the ground begins to shake beneath your tram, the street above gives way and a large tanker truck falls through. What company name is imprinted on the door of this truck?
    a. Olympic
    b. Ormond
    c. Olson
    d. Olvera

> ### Did you know?
> The Earthquake attraction resets in under fifteen seconds ready for the next tram of unsuspecting guests.

40. ★★★ As you approach Amity Island, you will find advertisements for boats for sale on the wall of the building on your right side. Which price is correct for the 90-foot houseboat?
    a. $243,500
    b. $234,500
    c. $253,400
    d. $235,400

> ### Did you know?
> The opposite side of Amity Island is the sea side town of Cabot Cove, Maine. The hometown of writer Jessica Fletcher on the long running television series, *Murder, She Wrote*.

41. ★★★ Find the sign for the bankruptcy sale on the side of the Amity hotel. On what date does this sale take place?
    a. July 20
    b. August 20
    c. June 20
    d. January 20

42. ★★ What is the name of the diver you see in the water trying to find the shark?
    a. Office James
    b. Officer Allen
    c. Officer Jeff
    d. Officer George

43. ★ What did director Steven Spielberg name the shark during the production of *Jaws*?
    a. Brian
    b. Bruce
    c. Benjamin
    d. Benedict

44. ★★ What nickname did the production team call the movie *Jaws* due to all of the problems they had on set with the mechanical shark?
    a. Flaws
    b. Chaws
    c. Thaws
    d. Paws

The Great Universal Studios Hollywood Scavenger Hunt

> **Did you know?**
> The Jaws attraction premiered on the backlot in 1976 after the block buster film *Jaws* took audiences by storm the year before.

45. ✯✯ As you tour continues, you will pass by a large white house on your right. This house is known as what sort of ranch?
    - a. Cattle
    - b. Horse
    - c. Chicken
    - d. Turkey

> **Did you know?**
> This white house is best known for the film *The Best Little Whorehouse in Texas* starring Dolly Parton and Burt Reynolds. This property is known as a practical set, which means the production crew can film on the inside, as well as the outside.

> **Did you know?**
> As your tour turns down Colonial Street, this was not the original location of this residential section of the backlot. Colonial Street originated near the New York street sets but was moved to this area to allow for more room to expand the metropolitan area.

> **Did you know?**
> As your tour turns down colonial street, notice the first house on your left side. This house was the sorority house in the classic comedy *Animal House* starring the late John Belushi.

> ### Did you know?
> You will find a large house with a porch that spans the entire front of the structure on your left side. This was the house of Gabrielle on the long running ABC show, *Desperate Housewives*.

46. ★★ Your tour guide will point out a house on your left that was the residence of what spooky family?
    a. The Addams Family
    b. The Munster's
    c. The Brady's
    d. The Partridge Family

> ### Did you know?
> The 1313 Mockingbird Lane house was also used as Elvira's home in the film *Elvira: Mistress of the Dark*.

> ### Did you know?
> Veteran actress Doris Day filmed in each of these houses on Colonial Street over the course of her career, each time with a different husband.

> ### Did you know?
> As you reach the end of Colonial Street you will find one home at the end and empty space surrounding. Previously this area was built to reflect a small town and town square area. This area was used in such classic television shows as *Leave it to Beaver* and *The Twilight Zone*.
>
> You may ever recognize the center grassy area as Fallwell Massachusetts from a lesser known film starring the mistress of the dark, Elvira of the same name.

The Great Universal Studios Hollywood Scavenger Hunt

> **Did you know?**
>
> As you continue your tour through Colonial Street, your tour guide will point out the houses from the ABC television show, *Desperate Housewives*.
>
> In the fourth season, this area was destroyed to resemble a tornado that hit the neighborhood causing severe damage to the structures and street area.

47. ☆ As you turn to the left off the main road, you will see the Bates Motel from the Alfred Hitchcock classic, *Psycho*. What is the first name of the man who runs this motel?
    a. Norman
    b. Norton
    c. Nathan
    d. Nelson

> **Did you know?**
>
> The Psycho house you pass with mother Bates in the window was once a part of Colonial Street. The house was moved to this location to preserve the creepy nature as the colonial street homes were changed and updated as needed for filming.

48. ☆ As your tour takes you to the plane crash site from the 2005 remake of *War of the Worlds*. What is the model airplane you see before you?
    a. 757
    b. 767
    c. 747
    d. 777

49. ☆☆ Your tour will take you near a large blue backdrop with a large pool in front of it. What is the name of the pool and backdrop area?
    a. Universal Lake
    b. Back drop Lake
    c. Jaws Lake
    d. Falls Lake

Did you know?

The Falls Lake backdrop was installed for the filming of *Jaws the Revenge*. The water was dyed blue to match the color of the water in the Caribbean. Unfortunately for the actors who were in the water, the dye turned their blonde hair bright blue also.

Some of your favorite films have used the Falls Lake area of Universal Studios Hollywood. Just a few of these famous films are: *Oh Brother, Where Art Thou, Van Helsing, Jurassic Park III, National Treasure II: Book of Secrets, Pirates of the Caribbean: Curse of the Black Pearl* and *Pirates of the Caribbean: On Stranger Tides*. Next time you have the chance to watch some of these films, see if you can spot Falls Lake.

Did you know?

As your tram turns the corner, you will see a log cabin near the street. This cabin was built for the film, *The Great Outdoors* starring John Candy and Dan Aykroyd. This location has also been seen in *The Naked Gun 33 1/3* and *Desperate Housewives*.

Did you know?

The area that now houses the Fast and the Furious: Supercharged attraction once was the home of the Ice Cave, and later, the Curse of the Mummies Tomb. This attraction would spin around the tram and give the illusion that the trams was turning within the tunnel.

The Great Universal Studios Hollywood Scavenger Hunt

Bonus Question

50. ★★★ How many films to date have been produced for *The Fast and the Furious* franchise?
    a. Six
    b. Ten
    c. Twelve
    d. Eight
51. ★★ Which member of the *Fast and the Furious* movies greets you when you enter the garage?
    a. Tej
    b. Roman Pierce
    c. Dominic Toretto
    d. Lettie
52. ★ What name does Roman refer to the vehicle built by Tej as your tram pulls into the parking garage?
    a. Marilyn Monroe
    b. Mona Lisa
    c. Virgin Mary
    d. Cleopatra
53. ★ When Lettie asks you to turn off camera's and cell phone she says, "one flash or _____ could give you away."
    a. Text
    b. Phone call
    c. Click
    d. Ring tone
54. ★★★ On the wall to the left of the tram in the first garage you will find a sign that reads, "Perez and _____."
    a. Sons
    b. Company
    c. Perez
    d. Hilton
55. ★★ As your tram pulls into the next bay, you come into a dance party. What breaks up the party?
    a. Gun shots
    b. The police
    c. The FBI
    d. The bad guys
56. ★★ When the agent says he's the one holding the gun, how does special agent Hobbs respond?
    a. You call that a gun
    b. Mine's a whole lot bigger than yours
    c. Yeah, but can you shoot it?
    d. That's a sissy gun

57. ★★★ What happens that tips off Shaw to your location?
    a. He hears the music
    b. Roman's phone rings
    c. Hobbs gun goes off
    d. He hears cars racing
58. ★★ When Shaw shows up and threatens the tram, he says, "Which one of you is the witness. Speak now or you all get _____."
    a. Fried
    b. Wasted
    c. Blasted
    d. Shot
59. ★★ As the chase begins, Roman and Lettie hook up the tram to their vehicles and Romans says, "I've got the _____."
    a. Tiger by the tail
    b. World on a string
    c. Bull by the horns
    d. Car by the wheels
60. ★★★ Lettie grabs Shaw's truck to stop him from threatening the tram, what does she say he should eat?
    a. Rubber
    b. Your words
    c. Pavement
    d. Asphalt
61. ★★ While Dom is hanging on the helicopter, he warns Lettie that there is a problem with the bridge you are about to cross. What is the problem he warns her about?
    a. The bridge is up
    b. It has been blown up
    c. Under construction
    d. Has been blocked
62. ★★ How does Dom say your tram will get across the bridge?
    a. Go faster
    b. Nitrous
    c. Drifting
    d. Hit the gas
63. ★★ As you fly through the air, Dom says, "Ride or _____."
    a. Die
    b. Live
    c. Fly
    d. Roll

The Great Universal Studios Hollywood Scavenger Hunt

Did you know?

As your tram works its way back to the unload area, this area once housed the Battlestar Galactica attraction. In 1979, Universal Studios created the Battlestar Galactica attraction with the popular Cylon guards. An actor would burst in and save the guests from annihilation just in time.

As you finish your tour of the Universal Studios Hollywood theme park, I hope you have seen the parks through new eyes. First time guests, my hope is to help you get the most out of your visit to this iconic theme park. Frequent visitors, if you found even two new items, I have succeeded in my mission.

My love of all of Universal Studios continues daily knowing a new thrill is waiting for me next time I visit the parks. Never would I want to have a day when I did not find something new to fall in love with at Universal Studios Hollywood.

Answer Key

Upper Lot

1. B – 1899
2. C – 1950's
3. A – Tuesday and Thursday
4. D – Actors
5. C – 1925

New York Street

6. B – One hundred fifty
7. C – Fire
8. D – Seventeen
9. A – Pennies
10. B – Unisphere
11. C – 28 Million
12. A – $1.25
13. C – Out of town calls
14. B – $5.40
15. D – Contender
16. A – Bread

17. D – 1956
18. C – Salesmen

Pets Place

19. C – 1936
20. D – Purple
21. C – Abigail
22. B – Firetruck
23. A – Hearts
24. C – *Little Red Riding Hood*
25. D – Groceries
26. C – 1887
27. A – Thirty-two
28. B – Toothpaste
29. D – Blueberry
30. A – Free
31. C – Twenty-two
32. D – Hairball
33. C – Dr. Francis
34. B – $15
35. D – Juggling
36. A – Count Lasagna on Red
37. C – Protection from the zombie apocalypse
38. D – One hundred fifty dollars
39. C – Seventy-five cents
40. B – A leash
41. B – Friday
42. A – Heavy metal
43. D – Cavalier King Charles
44. C – Make your own broom
45. B – Pet costume parade
46. A – Grapes
47. B – Ukulele
48. A – Hockey

The Great Universal Studios Hollywood Scavenger Hunt

49. D – Yellow
50. C – Sandwich
51. C – Dust
52. D – Floor food
53. B – Castle
54. A – Table scraps
55. B – Blue
56. C – Yellow
57. D – Bedroom linens
58. C – Pastrami on rye
59. A – Five minutes
60. B – Turtle
61. C – Dr. Theodora Carlton
62. A – Twenty-five
63. D – Cat-O-Matic
64. B – Chloe
65. A – Freedonia
66. B – Friday
67. D – Bruno's
68. C – Purple
69. C – A
70. A – Tiara
71. B – Blue
72. D – J
73. A – Green
74. C – Music

Paris Street

75. C – 40
76. A – Balard
77. D – Perfume
78. B – 1862
79. C – No smoking
80. D – A lighter

81. D – De La Fontaine
82. B – Casanova
83. C – Seven hundred

Despicable Me: Minion Mayhem

84. A – 1966
85. C – Missouri
86. D – Two Billion
87. B – He's not just a pretty face
88. D – Poison dart frogs
89. A – Leopold
90. C – Felonius
91. A – Bird
92. B – Alligator
93. D – Sock puppet
94. B – Three hours
95. D – The person wearing them
96. A – A fork
97. D – Dynamite
98. C – Banana
99. B – A cactus
100. C – Fly swatter
101. A – Yellow
102. D – Anti-gravity
103. C – Gru doll
104. B – Five
105. D – Seven

Super Silly Fun Land

106. A – Pink
107. A – Shark
108. D – Seven
109. B – A duck

DreamWorks™ Theater Featuring Kung Fu Panda

110. C – Pinocchio
111. A – *Dinosaur*
112. D – Po
113. A – *Shrek the Third*
114. B – *How to Train your Dragon*
115. C – *How to Train your Dragon 2*
116. D – *Shrek*
117. B – Rico
118. A – Macchiato
119. B – Blue
120. C – Thundering Rhino
121. D – Sword of Heroes
122. C – He read his mail
123. A – Ultimate power
124. B – Have a tea party
125. A – Master Shifu
126. B – Alex the lion
127. D – Skipper
128. C – Gumdrop buttons
129. B – Master Shifu
130. D – Waterfall
131. A – Bunnies
132. B – River pirates
133. C – Three
134. D – In the spirit realm
135. D – Mr. Ping
136. A – Po
137. B – Mr. Ping's secret ingredient hot sauce
138. C – His kung fu

Catherine F. Olen

Wizarding World of Harry Potter™

1. B – Halloween
2. C – 69.45
3. A – 24 February

Zonko's Trick's and Jokes

4. D – 5357
5. B – Duck
6. A – Monocle
7. B – Flies
8. C – Buffalo
9. D – Boomerang

Honeydukes™

10. B – Twenty
11. A – Twenty-four
12. D – Pumpkin cakes
13. D – Sixteen

The Three Broomsticks

14. B – Thirty-six

Hog's Head

15. C – Ale
16. A – Steak and Kidney pudding
17. A – The witching hour
18. C – Five
19. B – Your head
20. A – Doxy eggs
21. D – White rat whiskey
22. B – Zanzibar

The Great Universal Studios Hollywood Scavenger Hunt

23. D – Eighteen
24. C – Seventeen
25. A – Nine
26. B – Silver weed

Ollivanders™

27. B – 382 BC
28. A – The wand chooses the wizard

Owl Post

29. B – Two hundred fifty-seven
30. A – Permission form
31. C – Crystal
32. C – Violin
33. D – Cauldron

Dervish and Banges™

34. B – Bite
35. D – Cast a security spell
36. A – Horklump Juice
37. C – Nimbus 2000
38. A – Porcuquils
39. B – Abacus
40. D – Defense against the dark arts O.W.L.S.
41. B – Didn't come home for the holiday

Gladrags Wizardwear™

42. B – A cat
43. C – Rome
44. A – Tailoring

Tomes and Scrolls Specialist Bookshop

45. B – 1768
46. A – *Meandering with Mummies*
47. D – Fruit
48. C – Ten

Flight of the Hippogriff™

49. D – Pumpkin
50. A – The forest is forbidden to all students
51. C – Sirius Black
52. B – Norwegian Ridgeback

Harry Potter and the Forbidden Journey™

53. D – Erised
54. C – Neville
55. A – A scroll
56. D – Gryffindor
57. B – The owlery
58. A – 1709
59. D – Salazar Slytherin
60. B – The dark side
61. C – Lord Voldemort
62. D – What is easy
63. A – A few short hours
64. D – Cloak of invisibility
65. B – It's fascinating
66. C – See a game of Quidditch™
67. D – It starts snowing
68. B – Relive your worst memories
69. A – Happy memory
70. C – Dragon
71. D – Peter Jones

The Great Universal Studios Hollywood Scavenger Hunt

72. B – Hufflepuff and Gryffindor
73. A – Goblin
74. C – Wizard
75. B – Hermione
76. D – A metal chain and collar
77. A – The whoomphing willow
78. C – The great hall
79. D – Lord Voldemort
80. C – His glasses

Special Effects Show

1. B – Magic lantern
2. A – Hold on to your butts
3. C – A key
4. D – Real
5. C – Boris Karloff
6. B – *The Birds*
7. D – Their wearing nice pants
8. A – Actor
9. C – Over thirty
10. B – Lon Chaney
11. A – Chocolate syrup
12. D – Michael Meyers
13. C – Jamie Lee Curtis

Universal's Animal Actors

1. A – Chicken finger
2. B – Sparky
3. D – Treats
4. C – A dollar bill
5. B – Flap really hard and fly down to get it
6. D – Raptor
7. C – A giant fan

8. A – Mark
9. B – Brassiere
10. D – Jump over tires
11. C – Run a cat scan
12. B – Vegetarian sandwich
13. A – Fi Fi
14. C – Scene ten
15. D – Flipper
16. B – Flea Wars

WaterWorld®

1. D – Polar ice caps melted
2. A – Atoll
3. C – Helen
4. D – Pure dirt
5. B – The Deacon
6. B – Smokers
7. C – A golf club
8. A – The Provider
9. D – Build on it
10. C – Fish
11. B – Drop him in toxic waste
12. D – Husband and wife
13. A – Set him on fire

Springfield

1. C – The Stonecutters
2. D – Embiggens
3. B – 1796
4. A – Bi monthly Sci Fi Con
5. B – Zebra Girl
6. D – Krustylu Studios

The Great Universal Studios Hollywood Scavenger Hunt

7. C – #1DOOFUS
8. B – Nine

Krusty Burger

9. A – Nine
10. B – *Take my life, Please*
11. D – Three
12. C – Thanksgiving
13. A – Wiggum
14. D – *Funeral for a Friend*
15. B – The third-grade
16. D – *Mr. Plow*
17. C – Nahasapeemapetilons
18. A – *Kamp Krusty*
19. D – Buy this comic!
20. B – Ned Flanders
21. A – Luke Perry
22. B – Motion Sickness
23. C – Itchy
24. C – It's a long, long line!
25. C – Rodney Dangerfield
26. B – Michael Jackson
27. A – Wash his hair
28. D – Bender
29. C – Bette Midler
30. A – Stephen Hawking
31. B – Clown college
32. D – Gabbo
33. A – Bleeding Gums Murphy
34. C – Sideshow Bob
35. D – Marge
36. B – Murderer
37. A – Live

38. D – *New Kid on the Block*
39. C – New York
40. C – Barry White

Cletus Chicken Shack

41. A – Moonshine
42. C – Squirrel
43. D – Turkey
44. B – Spider Pig
45. C – Donkey
46. D – Twenty-five
47. B- Chicken thumbs
48. A – Day old beaks
49. C – Jeremy Freedman
50. A – Hans Moleman
51. D – Almost a burger
52. B – Mr. Largo

Moe's Tavern

53. D – Casanova
54. C – Grandpa Simpson
55. A – Shelbyvillians
56. B – Twenty-six
57. A – Pruno
58. C – Alkie's Choice
59. D – 24601
60. C – Thirty
61. C – Drunky
62. B – Smiling Joe Fission
63. A – Two
64. D – Gone fission
65. B – *The Itchy and Scratchy Movie*
66. A – Unlicensed

The Great Universal Studios Hollywood Scavenger Hunt

67. C – Eddie and Lou
68. B – Snake
69. D – *One Hit Wonder*
70. C – Jub-Jub
71. A – Sideshow Mel
72. C – Six hundred forty-seven
73. B – BLIND
74. D – Brandine Spuckler
75. A – Crazy old man
76. D – Patty and Selma Bouvier
77. C – 24601

The Kwik-E-Mart

78. A – Maggie
79. D – James Woods
80. B – Flesh eating bacteria
81. C – Chow Mein
82. C – Five pounds
83. A – Baby Gerald
84. A – Mango Chutney Explosion
85. D – Extra moss
86. B – Ten thousand years
87. C – The Flaming Moe
88. C – Snowball II
89. D – No out of state checks
90. A – Old
91. D – Your luck
92. A – Bart
93. C – Six
94. A – 77621
95. B – Homer Simpson

Catherine F. Olen

The Simpson's Ride

96. D – Itchy and Scratchy
97. C – Rip-off
98. D – Unhappy teen employees
99. B – Shame and rejection
100. A – Probed
101. B – Cletus
102. C – Sherri and Terri
103. D – McBain
104. C – Paris Texan
105. B – Yard work
106. D – Hans Moleman
107. D – Date with Moe
108. C – Tire yard
109. B – The Traumanator Coaster
110. A – Side Show Robert
111. C – Stingy candy
112. D – Fried sugar
113. C – Screamatorium of Dr. Frightmarestein
114. A – Krusty
115. D – Switch
116. B – Bellybutton
117. B – Mr. Burns
118. A – Groping undertaker
119. D – Annual ghostbusting
120. C – Five hours
121. B – Grapefruit
122. A – Hammer
123. B – Barf
124. D – Clown hair
125. C – Forty-five minutes
126. A – Nelson
127. C – Chain reactions

128. D – Killer whale
129. D – Maggie
130. B – Her pacifier
131. C – You don't know where they've been
132. A – Kang and Kodos
133. B – Bart Simpson
134. C – Eight
135. D – Smiling Joe Fission

Lower Lot

Revenge of the Mummy

1. B – Imhotep lives!
2. A – Sand
3. C – The riches of eternal life
4. D – Souls

Jurassic World

5. C – Komodo Dragon
6. B – 8,000 Newtons
7. D – Early Cretaceous
8. A – 308 pounds
9. B – 17.06 feet
10. C – Roofed lizard
11. A – Sixty-five million
12. D – Velociraptor
13. B – Chris Pratt
14. D – Sixty feet
15. C – Stegosaurus
16. A – Dilophosaurus
17. B – Blue

Catherine F. Olen

Transformers: The Ride 3D

18. A – Cybertronian
19. D – Security
20. C – Hero recruitment officer
21. D – Species
22. B – Bumblebee
23. A – Rampage
24. C – War
25. B – The AllSpark
26. D – A churro
27. C – Insects
28. A – Devastator
29. C – Beg for mercy
30. B – Bumblebee
31. D – Freedom fighters

The World-Famous Studio Tour

1. D – Jimmy Fallon
2. C – *Damon and Pythias*
3. A – 1923
4. B – Carl Laemmle
5. C – Bela Lugosi
6. A – Mae West
7. B – Woody Woodpecker
8. B – Boris Karloff
9. A – Jeepers
10. C – Seven
11. D – Alfred Hitchcock
12. C – John Belushi
13. A – Loni Anderson
14. B – Sean Penn
15. B – 1985

16. D – 2001
17. C – 65 million
18. A – Russell Crowe
19. A – A yoyo
20. C – Ray Charles
21. B – Everything
22. A – Oh brother
23. D – Dressing rooms
24. C – 5195
25. A – *Back to the Future*
26. C – Skull island
27. D – Tyrannosaurus Rex
28. B – Ferrari 308
29. C – Biff Tannen
30. A – Foot power
31. D – Ingen
32. B – Al Roker
33. C – Snow and sleet
34. D – Mercado
35. A – High
36. D – *All Quiet on the Western Front*
37. C – Court of miracles
38. B – San Francisco subway
39. D – Olvera
40. A – $243,500
41. C – June 20
42. D – Officer George
43. B – Bruce
44. A – Flaws
45. C – Chicken
46. B – The Munster's
47. A – Norman
48. C – 747

49. D – Falls Lake
50. D – Eight
51. B – Roman Pierce
52. B – Mona Lisa
53. D – Ring tone
54. A – Sons
55. C – The FBI
56. B – Mine's a whole lot bigger than yours
57. B – Roman's phone rings
58. A – Fried
59. C – Bull by the horns
60. D – Asphalt
61. C – Under construction
62. B – Nitrous
63. A – Die

www.ingramcontent.com/pod-product-compliance
Lightning Source LLC
Chambersburg PA
CBHW071243070526
44583CB00017B/2310